WOMEN OF FAITH™
STUDY GUIDE SERIES

MANAGING
YOUR MOODS

FOREWORD BY
MARY
GRAHAM

NELSON IMPACT
A Division of Thomas Nelson Publishers
Since 1798

www.thomasnelson.com

Published by Nelson Impact, a Division of Thomas Nelson, Inc., P.O. Box 141000, Nashville, Tennessee, 37214.

ISBN: 0–7852–5151–0

05 06 07 08–12

✦ CONTENTS ✦

✦ FOREWORD ✦

My mother had a lot to manage. As the youngest of her eight children, one of her greatest challenges must have been me. I was apparently a temperamental little thing with big mood swings. What I remember most is a range of feelings that completely preoccupied my internal world. I felt deeply all the time about everything. I felt mad, bad, sad, or glad. Those feelings came often and forcefully. My mother's response was very consistent: when I felt mad, bad or sad, I went straight to my room until I changed my mood to glad, whereupon I could instantly rejoin the huge crowd in the more public areas of our home.

I have to say that was very good experience in learning to control my emotions, but it didn't contribute to my mental health over the long haul. I've not always wanted, nor been able, to isolate myself until I feel good again.

As an adult, I've learned to be grateful for a full gamut of emotions. Marilyn Meberg has been a great teacher and friend in this regard. She's helped me understand God's design, and how He gave us tender hearts and caring ways of expression. She's helped me know that splitting off what some consider "negative" feelings can lead to despair and destruction. We were not made for that.

Through the years, when Marilyn senses my spirit in a downward spiral, far from sending me away, she pursues me. "Tell me how you are." "How did that feel?" How ya' doin'?" All questions I've heard a thousand times from Marilyn. Then she listens for hours if that's what it takes. And guess what? After those encounters, I feel understood, loved, and guess what? Better. I feel much better than when I isolate myself with my feelings. Usually those encounters end with both

Marilyn and me laughing our heads off at something. It's a very healing process. That's what friends are for.

Staying in community not only helps us feel better, it helps us not act out emotions in negative, destructive ways.

God has created us as emotional beings, capable of a wide range of feelings. Obviously, His desire is that those feelings do not control us. We have ways to keep our feelings in "check" (so the rest of the world can live with us regardless of how we feel!) God has given us His Spirit to control us, His Word to counsel us, and His People to console and comfort us.

As you work through the studies in these pages, be honest with yourself and your friends. Lean in to your feelings: the good, bad, and ugly. Talk about how you feel and why. Learn from this study God's perspective on our emotional lives and what He does to help us manage our moods. I think you'll find your feelings can be your allies. They'll take you to the Savior, drive you to His Word, and connect you with your friends. You'll be closer than ever to being all He created you to be.

—*Mary Graham*

✦ INTRODUCTION ✦

As you know, God created us with a broad spectrum of emotional potential. On one end of the spectrum, we experience giggles, gladness, and joy; on the other end, sadness, disappointment, and anger. It is important that we feel all of these emotions, and even express them, but by the same token, we must learn to express them in appropriate ways.

—Marilyn Meberg

As children, we learn the ability to read faces. A frowning face means someone is sad. A smiling face means a person is happy. An open mouth and raised eyebrows equal surprise. Red cheeks indicate embarrassment. Eyebrows drawn together show anger. Simple, right? Well, no, not really. Life is a little more complex. Our feelings don't just run in the glad, sad, mad range. There are also feelings of disappointment, fear, depression, loneliness, elation, irritation, awe, eagerness, anticipation, affection, longing, resentment, worry, grief, confusion, compassion, frustration, jealousy, guilt, ambition, pride, desire, nervousness, infatuation, admiration, curiosity, and love, just to name a few. What's more, our emotions rarely fit into just one of those categories. We usually have mixed emotions, conflicting emotions, or we jump from one to the other in a matter of moments. Moods are a very difficult thing to manage in any woman's life!

Most of us live at the mercy of our moods and emotions. "When we're up, we're up, and when we're down, we're down." We are at war within ourselves, battling our contradicting feelings. We can't control *what* we feel. We just feel. But God says we are wise if we learn to manage our reactions to people and circumstances and determine how much our emotions will influence our lives. Now, we're not here to deal with the really severe emotional disorders. They certainly exist, but we can leave those to the experts. What we're going to tackle in this study are the garden–variety moods and emotions women deal with every day. We all struggle with our tempers. We all know what it's like to be jealous, lonely, worried, and overwhelmed. We all battle with rebellious feelings, not wanting to do what God asks of us. It's part of being human. It's part of being a woman. Isn't it nice to know you're not alone?

*"Why do you let your emotions take over,
lashing out and spitting fire?"*

Job 15:12 MSG

CHAPTER 1

A BUNDLE OF EMOTIONS

"A GOOD MAN OUT OF THE GOOD TREASURE OF HIS HEART BRINGS FORTH GOOD; AND AN EVIL MAN OUT OF THE EVIL TREASURE OF HIS HEART BRINGS FORTH EVIL."

Luke 6:45

When we start talking about moods and emotions, we must begin with the heart. I guess you could say it's the heart of the matter! We call it the seat of our emotions, and we try to explain our feelings by referring to it. People can be described as hardhearted, softhearted, openhearted, warmhearted, coldhearted, fainthearted, or even heartless. Some people wear their heart on their sleeve. We know what it's like to lose heart, take heart, have our heart set on something, have a change of heart, and have our hearts skip a beat. We know what it's like to do something to our heart's content. We can be heavyhearted, halfhearted, or lighthearted.

CLEARING ✦ THE ✦ COBWEBS

We all feel such a wide range of emotions. As you begin this study, which of your moods and emotions most trouble you?

A story can be heartwarming, heart wrenching, or heartening. We can share from our hearts, set our hearts on a thing, learn something by heart, have our hearts in the right place, and win the hearts of others. We have known heartache. We have been heartsick. Some days, we don't have the heart to face our work. Other days, we tackle the job heartily, going at it heart and soul. Those we love are always close to our hearts. We have people who are dear to our hearts set our hearts at rest. We know the kinds of things that do a heart good. We have read God's Word and taken it to heart. We have given heartfelt thanks for the blessings we receive. We know, in our heart of hearts, the right thing to do. And I hope, from the bottom of my heart, you will follow after God with all your heart. Whew! How about a hearty *Amen* to that!

1. The Scriptures are filled with descriptions of our hearts. Have you ever noticed how many amazing adjectives are used to describe it—for good or for bad? Let's take a few minutes to match the passages with the words it uses to describe the attitudes found in our hearts.

___ Psalm 112:7	a. standing in awe
___ Psalm 119:80	b. merry
___ Psalm 119:161	c. blameless
___ Psalm 131:1	d. backslidden
___ Proverbs 14:14	e. steadfast
___ Proverbs 16:5	f. haughty or humble
___ Proverbs 17:22	g. noble and good
___ Luke 8:15	h. proud

2. The Bible talks a lot about the heart, and the emotions tangled up within it. God knows we all have our ups and downs. What two emotional extremes are mentioned in Proverbs 15:13?

3. What kinds of things are going on in our hearts, according to Proverbs 16:9?

4. The psalms are wonderful for giving us glimpses into the inner turmoil of the heart. David's honesty allows us to compare notes on the most intimate levels.

- In Psalm 25:17, what does David say his troubles have done?

- Why is David so concerned about keeping his heart pure, according to Psalm 66:18?

- What is the state of David's heart in Psalm 109:22?

We are moody people, as changeable as the weather. But because we're all so experienced in emotions, we know how to spot them. We can read faces. We can interpret body language. Usually, the attitude of our heart and the mood we are in come across loud and clear. Folks notice. Whether we realize it or not, we are being defined by the emotion we display most consistently. We'll make reference to the mood when we describe people to each other.

"She strikes me as a very nervous person."

"She's the clingy type."

"What a whiner!"

"Well, you know how possessive she is."

"She's a cold fish."

"She's so upbeat!"

"Such a worrier!"

"High–strung."

"Snob."

"Such a sweetheart."

"Always so bubbly."

We also notice changes in mood.

"What's gotten into her?"

"I wonder what's wrong with her today?"

Though we might try to hide our inner turmoil, our emotions leak out when we're with other people.

5. Our moods can affect us physically. How does David's distress affect him, according to Psalm 102:4?

6. Our emotions can prompt us into action. What tangle of feelings led Paul to write his letter to the church in Corinth in 2 Corinthians 2:4?

7. When we allow our feelings—like worry, fear, and doubt—to carry us along, how does James 1:6 describe us?

> *Talk about an unloader; David unloaded throughout the psalms. One of the reasons I so love his God–inspired writing is that he didn't hold or hide his emotions. I find the psalms therapeutic because whatever I may be feeling, I can find a psalm in which David expresses the same feeling.*
>
> Marilyn Meberg

8. We often say our goal should be to have the mind of Christ (Phil. 2:5). Now, there was a Man who was able to manage His moods! Jesus never allowed His feelings to lead Him into sin. Still, it's a comfort to know the LORD completely understands how we feel. How does Hebrews 4:14–15 describe Jesus' inner struggles while on earth?

9. Moods, emotions, feelings, attitudes of the heart—they are powerful and easily overrule what we know is the right thing to do. What exhortation does Paul make in Colossians 3:16 that can powerfully counteract the tugging of our hearts?

✦ DIGGING DEEPER ✦

The Berean church in Acts didn't "invent" Bible study (Acts 17:11). In fact, such commitment to knowing and heeding God's Word is nothing new. Let's take a look at another verse of Scripture that talks about the importance of allowing the Word to dwell in our hearts—this time from the Old Testament. What does Moses say in Deuteronomy 30:14?

✦ PONDER & PRAY ✦

In the days ahead, take time to ponder what is in your heart. Ask the LORD for a measure of detachment, so you can see the feelings that flit through your heart, the moods that shape your day, and the emotions that rule you. Tell the LORD what you are finding, and ask for His help in sorting out what you discover. Then, take some Scripture—perhaps some of this week's verses—and plant them in your heart. The heart is not easily swayed by swinging moods if it is the dwelling place of the powerful Word of God.

✦ TRINKETS TO TREASURE ✦

At the close of every Women of Faith conference, women are asked to play a little game of pretend. Each conference guest is asked to imagine a gift has been placed in her hands—one from each of the speakers—to serve as reminders of the different lessons shared. This study guide will carry on this tradition! At the close of each lesson, you will be presented with a small gift. Though imaginary, it will serve to remind you of the things you have learned. Think of it as a souvenir. Souvenirs are little trinkets we pick up on our journeys to remind us of where we have been. They keep us from forgetting the path we have traveled. Hide these little treasures in your heart, for as you ponder them, they will draw you closer to God.

When we think God's way, we not only become wiser but also emotionally steady. I don't know how you feel about that, but I'm ecstatic! Consider that together we can become— and are—influential women of faith, making amazing contributions to our families and to society.

Patsy Clairmont

✦ TRINKETS TO TREASURE ✦

Our moods affect our actions, our attitudes, and the people around us. Your gift this week is something to remind you about the complexity of the moods and emotions that are bound up in our hearts. It's a rubber band ball. Our hearts are just as complex—a bundle of emotions rather than those stretchy binders. And it doesn't take too much to make either one a tangled mess! Through careful study of God's Word, we'll attempt to unravel these feelings and avert a knotty catastrophe!

✦ NOTES & PRAYER REQUESTS ✦

CHAPTER 2

HAPPINESS AT ANY COST

"HE WHO IS OF A MERRY HEART HAS A CONTINUAL FEAST."

Proverbs 15:15

Though dozens of moods are available to women, we would all prefer to be in a good one. And though numerous emotions flit through our hearts every day, one feeling is esteemed more than all the others—happiness. We don't really mind what God has planned for us, so long as we are guaranteed happiness in the midst of it. We want to live happily ever after. And what keeps us happy? When things go our way. When everything runs smoothly in the direction we had hoped it would go, we are able to maintain a pleasant frame of mind. No bumps. No interruptions. No inconveniences. In order

CLEARING ✦ THE ✦ COBWEBS

What changes would be necessary in your life in order for you to live "happily ever after"?

to maintain our personal contentment, we begin to avoid situations that might compromise our happiness.

I want no regrets, so I will take no chances. I do not want to feel shame, so I will blend quietly into the crowd. I don't want to be disappointed, so I'll lower my expectations. I do not feel happy when I am confused, so I won't bother learning anything new. I do not wish to be embarrassed, so I will avoid speaking up. I don't want to experience sadness, so I will not allow myself to care. We set up emotional comfort zones and stay within them. No one can make us budge, not even the LORD. We create our own happy, little bubble—a safe haven, untouched by others. We take firm control so we can always be happy. Happiness—no matter what the cost.

> *The human heart is selfish, prefers its own way, fights being molded by God, and doesn't want to give in when we don't get what is "rightfully ours." We're stubborn, prideful, and strong—willed, and these unbecoming characteristics are most starkly revealed in our relationships.*
>
> Luci Swindoll

1. Our emotions can deceive us. Our own selfish desires attempt to overrule what our heads tell us is right. What does Deuteronomy 11:16 warn?

2. What does Jeremiah tell us about the human heart in Jeremiah 17:9?

3. Jeremiah further warns that people would rather listen to the dictates of their own evil hearts than listen to God (Jer. 16:12). What kinds of things come out of the heart, according to Mark 7:21–22?

> *Every good life is a balance of duty and bliss. We will be called upon to do things we would rather not. Sometimes people say, "Just follow your heart," but that isn't necessarily the right approach. We have to weigh decisions by mind and spirit and by the Word of God.*
>
> Barbara Johnson

4. Solomon was wise, even in matters of the heart. What does he say about our hearts in Proverbs 28:26?

"*I* just want to be happy." That's not so bad. That's not such an unreasonable desire, is it? Or is it not? When we place our own happiness as the highest goal in life, we do so at a great cost. In doing so, we decide our happiness is more important than anyone else's. This self–centeredness begins to skew our perceptions. We begin to insist on people jumping through our hoops. Everything should fall in line with our expectations. If we are not happy, then things need to change. It's all about me—my plan, my choice, my favorites, my best interests, my comfort, and my happiness.

What's worse, our happiness becomes more important than God's truth. The things He is asking in the Scriptures put a crimp in our style—they might just compromise our ultimate happiness. Convinced instead that God would want us to be happy, we begin to pick and choose the parts of the Bible we'll apply. We try to fit the Scriptures into our comfort zones. That's modular faith, and we're only deceiving ourselves. In so doing, we feel justified as we continue on the path to becoming little tyrants, little despots, and little gods.

5. So our hearts are deceitful. They can deceive us, so we can't trust them. What are we to do? Thankfully, God understands our hearts, even when they leave us confused. Look at these verses.

Isn't it a comfort to know that God's love is never miserly, never punishing of our secret, doubt–plagued thoughts? He will never pelt us in anger. He will never leave us, even when we whine and throw tantrums in our frustrations over what we don't like or don't understand. After all, he knows that we're just candy–tossing toddlers at heart.

Marilyn Meberg

• What is God able to see beyond, according to 1 Samuel 16:7?

• What does God know, according to Psalm 44:21?

• What does Jeremiah 17:10 say the LORD can do?

• In Hebrews 4:12, what is God's Word able to do in our hearts?

6. God knows your heart. So why not give it to Him? What does Proverbs 3:5 tell us to do—and not to do?

7. If we truly want God's help in managing our mish–mashed moods, He asks us to do…what? Check out Psalm 34:18.

8. We join David in praying, "Let the words of my mouth and the meditation of my heart be acceptable in Your sight, O LORD" (Ps. 19:14). Check out the following verses to see how this can come about?

• What must our prayer be, according to Psalm 51:10?

• No matter what we may have done, what does Ezekiel 18:31 say we can do?

• What does Hebrews 10:22 liken the changing of our hearts to?

9. Happiness should never be our ultimate goal. Rather, we should be looking for God to make us new and give us a pure heart. What does God promise in Ezekiel 36:26?

✦ DIGGING DEEPER ✦

There are lots of verses in the Bible that talk about God giving us a new heart, another heart, a willing heart. Deceitful though they are, our hearts can be stirred to do that which is good and right and useful to the LORD. Here are just a few of those verses:

- Exodus 35:21–22
- 1 Samuel 10:9
- 1 Chronicles 28:9

✦ PONDER & PRAY ✦

This week, pray for God to help you understand your own heart. Ask the LORD to bring its wily ways clearly to your attention. Then, as you see how easily your emotions can lead you into trouble, ask for the courage to stop following your heart everywhere it goes. Give up the impulse to put your happiness first, and place your trust in God and His Word instead. Depend on God to give you a new heart, and to stir your heart to do His will.

✦ TRINKETS TO TREASURE ✦

Our heart is deceitful. Sneaky as a snake. Crafty as a fox. Wiley as Wiley Coyote, and just as persistent in trying to get what it wants. To remind us of this, this week's trinket is a bar of soap. No matter how much we want for God to make us clean, our heart is as slippery as soap. If we keep this in mind, we can be on guard against the whims of emotion. When we are wise, we cannot be led astray by the wiles of the heart.

✦ NOTES & PRAYER REQUESTS ✦

_____

_____

_____

_____

_____

_____

_____

✦ Notes & Prayer Requests ✦

CHAPTER 3

TEMPER, TEMPER

"BETTER TO DWELL IN THE WILDERNESS, THAN WITH A CONTENTIOUS AND ANGRY WOMAN."

Proverbs 21:19

Our temper is most often compared to flames of fire. We say tempers flare. Anger smolders in our hearts. We harbor burning wrath, seething emotions. People who lose their tempers are called hotheads or are said to have a short fuse. Anger barely contained is said to be boiling near the top. And when we can't contain the anger any longer, we blow our top and sparks fly. In cartoons, we see the stages of building emotion. Shoulders hunch, fists clench, faces scrunch, teeth clench, color rises through the face, eyes become bloodshot, steam begins to escape through the ears, and then comes the explosion. There are lots of ways to give vent to anger. We grit our teeth, we give someone "the look," we pull our hair, we jump up and down, we say hateful

CLEARING ✦ THE ✦ COBWEBS

What causes you to lose your temper? The big things? Or the little things?

things, we kick and scream, and we rant and rave. In any given household, there will be some combination of shouters, pouters, screamers, sulkers, snubbers, stompers, and sarcastics. Sounds like a soap opera or a sitcom, doesn't it?

By the time we hit kindergarten (give or take a year), most little people learn that temper tantrums are not acceptable. We urge them to exercise a little self–control. In order to stem the tide of fury, we are admonished to think before we speak, cool down, count to ten, and find healthy ways to express our frustration. But some of us never learn to control our tempers. It's one of the most unmanageable moods we face.

1. Anger unleashed almost always leads to feelings of regret. When we lose our temper, we often do and say things we wish we hadn't. We're far from alone in our struggles with our tempers. Many people in the Bible said words in the heat of the moment. Many of them behaved in ways they would later regret. Shall we take a look?

- What did Moses do in a fit of anger in Exodus 32:19?

- What was one man's perverse response in Numbers 22:27, just because he became frustrated and embarrassed?

- What false accusation was made by an angry brother in 1 Samuel 17:28?

- What shocking insults were flung in a moment of fury in 1 Samuel 20:30?

- What rash promise did David make when he was stirred up, according to 2 Samuel 12:5?

- Who threw a temper tantrum in Esther 1:12 when he didn't get his way?

- We are all apt to say unwise things when upset. How does Jonah react to God's reasonable question in Jonah 4:9?

2. What does Proverbs 14:29 tell us about people who cannot control their tempers?

3. How does Proverbs 29:22 characterize an angry man or woman?

So many people walk through life with regret. That seems like such a wasted, draining emotion to me. We are not powerless in our lives to make change, to start over again, to learn to do better next time.

Sheila Walsh

4. I once read your life is in the hands of any fool who can make you lose your temper. Read Ecclesiastes 7:9. What does Solomon call a person who is easily angered?

*ave you ever stopped to think about why we get angry? What's at the root of our basic temper tantrum? It's easiest to discern the heart of the matter with children. They pitch a fit when they want something and we tell them "no." They set up a howl when it's time to go home, because they'd rather continue having fun. They use angry words when they want their own way. Selfishness is at the root of their targeted tirades.

> *Think of the times you become angry or out of control. What's happening? Do you feel safe and secure? Do you feel competent and confident? Do you have faith that God is in perfect control of your life? I don't think so.*
>
> Thelma Wells

Are we so different? We get angry when we are inconvenienced. We get upset when we are disappointed, frustrated, and impatient. We lose our temper when people disobey us (when we don't get our way). Some of us get into the habit of anger because we've learned it's the fastest way to get what we want. We've learned it's a handy tool, because many people will relent, just to appease us. We're still losing our temper for entirely selfish reasons, even though we're adults.

5. Okay. That's all pretty clear. Losing our temper is a bad thing, and we should not let anger control us. Any advice on how that is done? Take a look at these three verses—what word is used for dealing with anger in each?

• Psalm 37:8

• Ephesians 4:31

• Colossians 3:8

6. So does that mean we can *never* be angry—that *all* anger is a sin? Well, no. Let's look at what Psalm 4:4 says?

7. It's impossible to say, "I will never be angry again." We need to set a realistic goal for ourselves. In Nehemiah 9:17, one of God's character traits is being "slow to anger." That's the ticket! What does Proverbs 16:32 consider praiseworthy?

> *Many Christians believe anger is an ungodly and unsanctified emotion and must never be felt, much less expressed. Yet Paul said in Ephesians 4:26, "Be angry and sin not" (KJV). We do not sin when we feel anger; we sin when we express it inappropriately.*
>
> Marilyn Meberg

✦ DIGGING DEEPER ✦

The Bible is full of wisdom and practical advice when it comes to anger. Here are several passages that encourage us with needed insights:

- Proverbs 15:1
- Proverbs 19:11
- Ephesians 4:26
- Proverbs 15:18
- Proverbs 22:24

✦ PONDER & PRAY ✦

When we delve into the moods and emotions that influence our lives, anger is not difficult to spot. But it can be very difficult to let go of. None of us want to say or do things that we'll live to regret. This week, pray for God's mercy and help as you deal with the anger harbored in your heart. Ask the LORD to make you more like Him—slow to anger and full of mercy.

> *"LORD, what do I do here?" I cried, "I'm angry. Please help me." At that moment, I made a conscious, determined choice to get on my knees and let my anger go. As I released my fury, I was filled with joy.*
>
> Sheila Walsh

✦ TRINKETS TO TREASURE ✦

Your little gift this week is a firecracker. Too often we'll use any excuse to light the flame on a short fuse. Even the littlest things set us off, and we explode before we even give a thought to what we're doing. Let this little firecracker remind you to watch your temper, because it can be a dangerous, little thing. When we do and say things in the heat of the moment, we can inflict a lot of damage.

✦ NOTES & PRAYER REQUESTS ✦

_____

_____

_____

_____

_____

_____

_____

✦ Notes & Prayer Requests ✦

CHAPTER 4

THE GREEN–EYED MONSTER

"WRATH IS CRUEL AND ANGER A TORRENT, BUT WHO IS ABLE TO STAND BEFORE JEALOUSY?"

Proverbs 27:4

Even though children are all very different from one another, they are very concerned with equality. If one chooses red for his or her new jacket, they all want red jackets. We can track years in the photo albums by what color jacket our kids are wearing. "Oh yes, that's the year they all had blue polar fleece!" If one child receives an apple, they all expect apples. Pies and pizzas must be divided with precision, so no one has a bigger piece than anyone else. The worst complaint they can bring against each other is inevitably accompanied by the resentful wail, "It's not fair!" Though it's a relief that the kids can usually agree on what's fair, I know very well the root of their obsession is *not* a desire for

CLEARING ✦ THE ✦ COBWEBS

Why do you think the grass is always greener in somebody else's yard?

justice. Far from it! They're nitpicking and weighing and comparing everything that comes their way because they are greedy at heart and jealous of one another. It sounds terrible, but it's just part of their nature as children.

Jealousy—it's the green–eyed monster. Solomon says, "Anger is cruel, and wrath is like a flood, but who can survive the destructiveness of jealousy?" (Prov. 27:4 NLT). It's an emotion that doesn't fade away when we grow up. We still have a tendency to wail, "It's not fair!" when life doesn't give us what we think we deserve. Even Christians are susceptible to pangs of jealousy. We are green with envy when it seems God has blessed other people more than we have been blessed. We resent this one's bigger house or that one's new car. We wonder why some women are so wise, poised, and articulate. This one is pretty. That one has the perfect career. This one has such polite children. That one has so many friends. Women who have to work are envious of women who are able to stay home with their kids. Women who stay home are jealous of women who have satisfying careers. Women who don't have children are jealous of the mothers with their babies, and mothers with big broods cast longing eyes at the woman who is free to do what she likes. Such foolishness!

I've learned that when I don't enter into my friends' successes with joy, it's usually because I'm jealous. Ouch...that's painful to confess...even to myself. Jealousy is like a spider's web. It's difficult to see its slender fibers, easy to get entangled in, and hard to brush off.

Patsy Clairmont

1. Envy is like a disease. How does Solomon say it affects us in Proverbs 14:30?

2. Jealousy brings with it other emotions—envy, resentment, bitterness, covetousness. When these forms of jealousy overtake our hearts, it shows itself in subtle—and not so subtle—ways.

- Why is greed sometimes difficult to discover, according to Luke 11:39?

- What does Psalm 101:5 say comes out of the mouth?

- And what speech is spoken of in Proverbs 25:23?

- Greed and envy become the habit of a heart. How does Peter describe such a one in 2 Peter 2:14?

3. Covetousness is such a danger to our hearts that God included it in the Ten Commandments. "You shall not covet your neighbor's house; you shall not covet your neighbor's wife, nor his male servant, nor his female servant, nor his ox, nor his donkey, nor anything that is your neighbor's" (Ex. 20:17). What are some of the consequences of covetousness, according to Proverbs 15:27 and Habakkuk 2:9?

4. What is the alternative to covetousness, according to Psalm 119:36?

5. And just what does God's Word tell us to do? Solomon says, "the righteous gives and does not spare" (Prov. 21:26). How does this giving attitude play itself out, according to 1 Corinthians 10:24 and Philippians 2:4?

In the Christian walk, we are told to love one another. Jesus, Paul, Peter, Matthew, Mark, Luke, John, and James—they all say the same thing. "I did not come to be served, but to serve." "Love your neighbor as yourself." "Consider one another." "Giving preference to one another." It's all so incredibly noble.

But at some point, doesn't it all just sound like lip service? Don't you ever have the urge to shout, "Hey! What about me? How do I know my needs will be taken care of?" If we're spending so much time being self–sacrificing, won't people just walk all over us? Won't we be taken for granted? No one else in the house seems to be grateful that toilet paper rolls are changed, empty ice cube trays are filled, and clean socks magically appear in dresser drawers. Who else refills the copier machine, replenishes dwindling office supplies, and empties the trash?

It's only after I've exhausted myself with indignation over how much I do that I realize something: Everyone feels this way. We all believe our efforts go unnoticed. And that's when I pray, *Oh God, give me a servant's heart. Because I want to be like You. And I know You see, even when no one else does.*

6. You have to love Martha! Here's a woman who wasn't afraid to march into a room full of people (who were just sitting around until supper was ready) and give voice to the feeling I often find in my heart. "Hey! What about me?" What does she say to Jesus in Luke 10:40?

7. Right up there with "What about *me*?" is the related query, "Hey! What about *her*?" Who asks that question in John 21:21, and how does Jesus wisely answer it in verse 22?

> I recall times of jealousy toward those closest to me, hating it in myself but seemingly unable to rise above it. I would pout, walk out, ignore, speak out of turn—in short, act like a petulant child.
>
> Luci Swindoll

8. We should never allow that green–eyed monster of jealousy to cause our eyes to wander from the task God has set before us. We each must answer for ourselves before the LORD. What does Paul say about this in Colossians 3:8?

> *I am a very human being.*
> *Each of us carries within*
> *us falsehood,*
> *self–centeredness,*
> *cowardice, and the*
> *capacity to do unbelievably*
> *unkind things to others.*
>
> Luci Swindoll

9. Let's not compare. Let's not covet. Let's not set up a wail of "It's not fair!" You will be rewarded according to your own labor. Let's leave the decision about what's fair to the LORD. What does Paul say in Galatians 6:4, 5?

✦ DIGGING DEEPER ✦

Some sins seem harmless enough. Who cares if we wish we had something that belongs to another? Nobody can see it. Nobody will know. But the greed we hide reveals a heart that is self–seeking, ungrateful, and covetous. God sees. God knows. And He takes these things very seriously. Just take a look at the sins God ranks right next to covetousness in the Scriptures. They'll make you cringe!

- 1 Corinthians 5:10, 11
- Ephesians 5:5
- 1 Corinthians 6:10
- 1 Timothy 3:3

✦ PONDER & PRAY ✦

This week's prayer must be to root out the green-eyed monster from our hearts. Jealousy, envy, covetousness, resentment, and the urge to shout, "Hey! What about me?"—Have they been a prominent part of your moods lately? Remind yourself that you will only have the LORD to answer to in the end—same as everybody else. Pray for God to help you quench the urge to compare. Ask for a generous spirit. Ask for a pure servant's heart.

✦ TRINKETS TO TREASURE ✦

We've got to keep those green eyes from wandering. And we've got to keep our eyes on our own lawns. With that in mind, your trinket for the week is grass seed! It's really quite easy to grow, even in a pot on the corner of your desk or on your kitchen windowsill. Just keep it "mowed" with your scissors! And all the while you're clipping and snipping, remember that the pruning and shaping taking place in every life is between that individual and the LORD. And just for laughs, remember what Chuck Swindoll says about the grass being greener in your neighbor's yard: Their water bill is probably higher!

✦ Notes & Prayer Requests ✦

CHAPTER 5

LONELY HEARTS

"LO, I AM WITH YOU ALWAYS, EVEN TO THE END OF THE AGE."

Matthew 28:20

When we moved a few years ago, it didn't take us very long to find a new church home. What did take a while, though, was fitting in. Where we had attended previously, everyone knew us. We had shared experiences. We had shared laughter and tears. We had known our niche in the congregation. Starting over was hard. Nobody knew our story. Nobody knew our gifts. Nobody knew our talents, skills, likes and dislikes. And because nobody knew us, we felt like a bunch of nobodies. The people in our new church seemed to have it all covered. They didn't need us. I mean, you can't just march into a Sunday school classroom on your first week visiting and say, "Hi! I'm so–and–so, and I have the gifts of helps, organization, and

CLEARING + THE + COBWEBS

Do you like to spend a lot of time by yourself, or would you rather be surrounded by people?

mercy. I'm renowned for my fudge brownies, and I used to head up our old church's nursing home ministry. Do I fit in here?"

Over the first several months of settling in, I struggled with loneliness. Not that I was alone. I had my family, and we'd begun attending a Sunday school class. It wasn't homesickness either—the desire to go back to where we had been. It was a loneliness to know and be known. I wanted to put names to all the faces in the crowd and have them know my name too. I wanted my pastor to know how much I respected him and that I was taking his sermons to heart. I wanted the women in the kitchen to know I enjoyed baking, and would love to help out. I wanted people to find out what I was like and then to like me. I didn't want to remain just another face in the crowd.

> Loneliness and isolation abound in the world, right in our neighborhoods, perhaps in our own homes. We all carry secrets—painful secrets that make us feel scared, alone, and sometimes alienated. Just being human means we often feel solitary or even rootless at the core of our being.
>
> Luci Swindoll

1. "I've known drudgery and hard labor, many a long and lonely night without sleep, many a missed meal, blasted by the cold, naked to the weather" (2 Cor. 11:27 MSG). Paul knew loneliness. Does it seem strange that an apostle, a pillar of the faith, could feel this way?

2. There is a lonely feeling to David's words in Psalm 69:20. Why does he wish he had someone to talk to?

3. In Genesis, God declared, "It is not good that man should be alone" (Gen. 2:18). In that context, God was talking about a man and a woman. But in general, God made us to need one another. What does Ecclesiastes 4:9–11 say one friend can do for another?

4. There are those of us who are alone most of the time. Paul uses the example of the widow. What does 1 Timothy 5:5 say this lonely woman can do?

5. Our hearts are lonely to know and be known, and there are times when we just need to get some things off our chest. We need an understanding ear to listen as we pour out our hearts. When times like that come, what does David say to do in Psalm 62:8?

*H*ow do you cultivate a friendship? It isn't always easy. First, you have to find someone who wants a good friend. So many women are already linked up with friends, so it might take some time. Then, you have to find out about each other—personality, background, beliefs, likes, trustworthiness. Let's face it. We don't always "click" with each other. It takes a lot of time to really bond, but over the course of months and years, friendship grows. There are ups and downs to share—listening, laughter, tears, encouragement, grief, prayers, misunderstandings, and forgiveness. Before you know it, you are giggling over private jokes, finishing each other's sentences, guessing what the other will order off a menu, and you can't imagine letting a day go by without checking in with each other.

> *David had a candid relationship with God. He told God exactly how he felt all the time, holding nothing back. This kind of vulnerability reflects David's tremendous security in God's constancy.*
>
> Marilyn Meberg

We believers are offered this kind of close bond as well. Jesus called His disciples "friends," and He extends to us the same invitation. Have you ever considered sharing things with the LORD you'd normally tell a girlfriend? Have you pursued your Savior through the Scriptures so that you know Him better than anyone else? Wouldn't it be wonderful to leave loneliness behind forever, knowing that God is always near, always faithful, and always ready to listen? That's a friendship worth cultivating!

6. Paul says we are not alone. Who is with us, according to 2 Corinthians 13:11 and Philippians 4:9?

7. That's not all! Who is with us according to 2 Thessalonians 3:16 and 2 Timothy 4:22?

8. Here's another! What does John 14:16, 17 say abides with us?

Have you been down in the mouth lately? Want to do something fun or uplifting for your spirit, but find yourself with no money to splurge? Ask God for a creative idea. He will give you one, and you will experience a dimension of his giving that is different from the rest.

Luci Swindoll

9. God is with us. Jesus is with us. The Spirit is with us. What more could we ask? And yet look at these three encouraging verses. What does each of them say is also with us?

- 2 Corinthians 13:14

- Colossians 2:5

- 2 John 1:3

✦ DIGGING DEEPER ✦

During His three years of ministry on the earth, Jesus didn't try to go it alone. He surrounded himself with disciples and friends. Yet look at John 8:29 and John 16:32. When it came right down to it, did Jesus say, "Oh, I was never alone because I had my buddies"? When the disciples abandoned Him, did He feel alone? What was Christ's attitude?

✦ PONDER & PRAY ✦

As you ponder and pray over the week ahead, ask the LORD to help you to grasp Whose you are, Who goes with you, and the gifts that abide with you because of that. Thank God for the blessings of friendship and look for ways to reach out to others this week. Be that listening ear, be the one with the encouraging word, be the one to hear and know and understand.

✦ TRINKETS TO TREASURE ✦

Your trinket for the week is a braided cord. A single strand of fiber might be fragile on its own, but it is strengthened when it is wound together with others. When our hearts are lonely, we realize how much the bonds of friendship mean. And when we have no other friends, how much more tightly we must weave our lives together with Jesus'! He is a Friend who can lift our hearts out of loneliness, for He knows us and loves us and encourages us to cultivate a friendship with Him.

✦ NOTES & PRAYER REQUESTS ✦

_____

_____

_____

_____

_____

_____

_____

✦ Notes & Prayer Requests ✦

CHAPTER 6

WORRIES AND FEARS

"DO NOT FRET—IT ONLY CAUSES HARM."

Psalm 37:8

hat do I need to worry about today? The dogs need walking, the kids will want breakfast, Laurie wants to have coffee and talk about her new beau, I have a couple of bills to pay, gotta pull something out of the freezer for supper, and there's time for a chapter or two in Philippians. The car needs gas, and oh, I almost forgot, I have to finish that spreadsheet for tomorrow's finance committee meeting. I'll need to oversee homework, get supper on the table, and (oh my goodness!) I should really brush my hair. Don't I have an appointment with the manicurist today? Aren't the Johnson's coming for dinner tomorrow night? That doesn't sound so bad, does it? When I take one day at a time, life looks like a piece of cake! But more often then not, my mind is stretching forward, and I

CLEARING
✦ THE ✦
COBWEBS

What one thing do you worry about the most?

begin to worry about my tomorrows. Don't you? I hope it doesn't rain for Saturday's game. I hope my new boss isn't a tyrant. I hope whoever buys the house next door doesn't have any rowdy teenagers. Do I need to get a part–time job to make ends meet? I'll bet all the kids will need braces. What if the house burns down? What if the plane crashes? I wonder if we have enough life insurance? What if I lose my job? What if it's cancer? Will we ever pay off the second mortgage? Do we have enough money for retirement?

Sure we need to plan ahead, but don't go borrowing trouble from tomorrow! If we allow our stomachs to roil over all the possibilities the future may hold, we'll make ourselves absolutely sick. Jesus wasn't kidding when He said not to worry about tomorrow because today has enough worries of its own. It's a good start on managing our anxious moods.

There are times you might be so fearful that all you can say is, "LORD, I'm scared. Please give me peace, because I am placing my trust in you. I know you can meet me right here. Please do!" And he will. He will enter into your mind and calm you with his presence.

Luci Swindoll

1. What does David say about his worries and fears in Psalm 55:4?

2. We may try to hide our fears, but what does David invite God to do in Psalm 139:23?

3. And what can we do when we are afraid, according to Psalm 56:3?

> *My sense of drama increases at night. I'm not sure what that's about, but the nighttime hours can seem longer, sadder, scarier, and lonelier than daytime hours.*
>
> Patsy Clairmont

4. God assures us that we don't have to worry. Let's look at a few of the things we don't need to worry about:

- Psalm 91:5

- Psalm 112:7

- Matthew 6:31

- Matthew 6:34

5. In today's world, with the news we hear from around the world, it's easy to get tense about our safety. There are new diseases cropping up. There are whole nations out there who hate us. We are always hearing about security risks, national alerts, and death threats. What was David's advice in Psalm 37:1?

ear is an emotion that we've all encountered. Even the bravest woman has felt the quiet gnawing of fear in her heart. It's wondering what might happen. It's knowing things are out of our hands. It's losing control. It's expecting the worst. It's having the jitters. It's losing our appetite. Queasiness. Sweating palms. Jangling nerves. Furrowed brow. Trembling hands. Pounding heart. Shortness of breath. Butterflies in the stomach.

When worry, anxiety, fretting, and fear overwhelm our hearts and minds, we tend to forget everything else. But God wants us to remember one very important thing—Him. When fears press in around you, cling to God. Hang onto His promises for you. Hold tight to hope. Trust God with your very life, and your faith will drive out the fears.

> *I couldn't allow my fluttering heart to determine what I would or would not do. So what if my hands trembled, my eye twitched, or my palms moistened? Most victories come with a price tag attached. Besides, momentary physical and emotional quivering seems like a small price to pay for building internal strength.*
>
> Patsy Clairmont

6. Here's a proverb for the anxious. What does Proverbs 12:25 warn us may happen if we continue to worry?

7. What good word can we share with a friend who is struggling with fear, according to Isaiah 35:4?

> *I have envisioned certain fears that I kept trying to keep ahead of, only to find that when I stopped and faced them, there was really nothing to fear at all.*
>
> Marilyn Meberg

8. Psalm 37:7 says, "Do not fret because of him who prospers in his way, because of the man who brings wicked schemes to pass." What attitude should we cling to instead, according to Psalm 56:4?

9. Jesus left this earth for a time. He promised He would return. But in the meantime, He left us a gift. What is that gift, according to John 14:27?

✦ DIGGING DEEPER ✦

Jesus said to His disciples, "Let not your heart be troubled; you believe in God, believe also in Me" (John 14:). Trusting Jesus does much to dispel our fears. Holding on to God's promises drives worries away. Let's look at just a few more of the verses in the New Testament that urge us to hold fast:

- 1 Corinthians 15:2
- 1 Thessalonians 5:21
- 2 Timothy 1:13
- Hebrews 10:23

- Philippians 3:12
- 1 Timothy 6:19
- Hebrews 3:6

✦ PONDER & PRAY ✦

Use your prayer times this week to talk over your fears with the LORD. Then, search the Scriptures for the various promises God has made to you as a believer. Rather than harboring worry and fear in your heart, begin planting these promises in their place. Then trust God to keep His word.

The LORD has given those of us who are fretters some prescriptions and promises that will help to soothe our ruffled minds in our darkest nights.

Patsy Clairmont

✦ TRINKETS TO TREASURE ✦

Though we may guard against it, sometimes our hearts are clutched by fear. Your trinket for this week is a butterfly—like the butterflies that get into our stomachs. God doesn't want us to be ruled by fear, but to trust in Him for all we need. He wants to transform our hearts and our lives, like the caterpillar that becomes a butterfly. So let go of worry, and let your heart soar!

✦ NOTES & PRAYER REQUESTS ✦

✦ Notes & Prayer Requests ✦

CHAPTER 7

THE DOLDRUMS

"WE DRY UP LIKE AUTUMN LEAVES—SIN—DRIED, WE'RE BLOWN OFF BY THE WIND."

Isaiah 64:6 MSG

Imagine being at sea. Not in some glamorous cruise ship with deck chairs and midnight buffets. No, this would be an old ship. The hull is patched tight with tar and pitch. The decks are rough wood, worn smooth by the daily scouring of salt water and the constant tread of bare feet. The sky is brilliant blue, cloudless. You are surrounded by the smells of saltwater, fish, and sweat. It's hot, for the sun is high and there is no wind. The big canvas sails hang limp from the masts. There's no breeze, not even a stirring of air. The sea is becalmed—still as glass in every direction. All around you the sailors are unnaturally quiet. They look restless, but oddly listless as well. The captain paces, stopping periodically to squint up into the sky. It's the dreaded doldrums.

CLEARING ✦ THE ✦ COBWEBS

What helps to shake you out of boredom?

For four days your ship has been trapped in a calm. No wind to move you forward, no currents to drift you along. Water is being rationed, and your mouth is dry as cotton. The only thing your ship can do is wait. Wait and pray for the wind.

Those are the real doldrums, but we borrow the term today. In every Christian's life, there are dry spells, times of dullness, seasons of waiting. Often, the doldrums come when we've gotten burnt out. Spiritual exhaustion that leaves us uncaring, listless, and longing for a breeze to refresh us.

Let's get reacquainted with ourselves. We've been dulled by life and all our responsibilities. We're reacting to our circumstances instead of purposefully engaging them.

Nicole Johnson

1. Have you ever felt spiritually stranded? Have you had that "blah" mood descend, and found it impossible to shake? David shares his misery in Psalm 6:6. What does he say on the matter?

2. Dry seasons come, even to those who love God. In the Old Testament, Solomon says such times dry the bones. What brings on the dryness, according to Proverbs 17:22?

3. Another word to describe life's doldrums is a feeling of dullness. Take a look at these verses. They give us some insight about what brings on the doldrums.

- Why have the shepherds in Jeremiah 10:21 become dull–hearted?

- In Acts 28:27, the people have grown dull because they are avoiding what?

- And in Hebrews 5:11–14, why have the people become dull of hearing?

4. One of the hardest things the LORD asks us to do is wait. We would rather have our answers now so we can move along. But God finds periods of waiting on Him are very beneficial. Still, just because we know something is good for us, it doesn't always mean we like it! What was David's reaction to waiting on the LORD in Psalm 69:3?

5. But there is help for us while we wait. What does Romans 8:26 encourage us with?

I love plants. My home and office wouldn't seem quite the same without green things scattered about. I've had ivies, ferns, gardenias, cyclamen, ficus trees, lemon trees, peace plants, palms, shamrocks, and sweet potato vines. Over the years I've had varying degrees of success with these plants, mainly because I sometimes forget to water them. Now, a plant can get along okay without spritzing and dusting and fertilizing, but when you forget to water it, it just shrivels up and dies. The end. That's why most of my plants are philodendrons. They're virtually indestructible. They even bounce back if you forget to water them for a week or so. They take my absentmindedness in stride.

> *God will deepen our faith, cultivate our character, and water our parched hearts.*
>
> Patsy Clairmont

Sometimes, I think my heart is like a philodendron, because I don't always take good care of it. It gets dusty with disuse, and I forget to feed it. Worse, I withhold it from God, and it suffers times of drought. But whenever I come to my senses and return to the LORD, my heart is soaked in living water and revives.

6. What does Isaiah 44:3 say will happen to those who are thirsty?

7. God "rekindles burned–out lives with fresh hope" (1 Sam. 2:8 MSG). What does Jeremiah 31:25 say that God can do?

God's Word works its invisible power over us in ways that can be subtle or overwhelming. It changes our moods, reworks our attitudes, and infuses us with courage. We inhale God's love and exhale His goodness, breathe in His grace, and breathe out His praise.

Barbara Johnson

8. According to Isaiah 40:29, God "energizes those who get tired, gives fresh strength to dropouts" (MSG). What does Jesus offer to the weary heart in Matthew 11:28, 29?

9. No matter how long you seem to be stuck in the doldrums, don't lose faith in God's ability to answer and refresh. Why does David say he never lost heart, according to Psalm 27:13?

✦ DIGGING DEEPER ✦

One of the words Jesus often uses is "Come." It is a word of invitation. The LORD calls to us and asks us to join Him. The following verses will help us understand what that means.

- Matthew 14:29
- Matthew 19:21
- John 1:39, 46
- John 6:44
- John 11:43

- Matthew 19:14
- Luke 19:5
- John 6:37
- John 7:37
- John 21:12

✦ PONDER & PRAY ✦

Are you in a season of dryness? Do you feel as if you're stranded in your spiritual walk and you long to move forward? Fill your prayers this week with pleas for refreshment, revitalization, and revival. Ask God to stir your heart, to stir up your hunger for His word, to stir up your thirst for righteousness.

✦ TRINKETS TO TREASURE ✦

Your little treasure for this week is a small watering can. It can serve to remind you of the importance of keeping your heart fed and watered. Don't let it get dusty; don't let it dry out. Saturate yourself with the Word of God. Turn to Him daily for the strength and life only He can supply. Let the LORD refresh your heart.

✦ NOTES & PRAYER REQUESTS ✦

✦ NOTES & PRAYER REQUESTS ✦

CHAPTER 8

SCATTERED

"MY SPIRIT IS OVERWHELMED WITHIN ME; MY HEART WITHIN ME IS DISTRESSED."

Psalm 143:4

We all know what it means to scatter something. Scattering is haphazard sprinkling. Lots of things scatter. We say we've had a scattering of snow. We scatter fertilizer on our lawns. Chickens scatter when a hawk flies overhead. In one of Jesus' parables, He talks about the sower scattering seeds in a field. We talk about scattered rain in the forecast, scattered clouds in the sky, scattering confetti at a party, and scattering pearls before swine. We have scatter rugs in our homes, and sometimes we need to gather together our scattered thoughts before we can speak.

Sometimes, I can be pretty scatter–brained, but when it comes right down to it, I don't *like* things scattered. I don't like my house scattered with clutter. I don't

CLEARING ✦ THE ✦ COBWEBS

What kinds of things should be avoided when you're emotionally distraught? Major decisions? Expensive purchases? Haircuts?

> *Sometimes the concept of rest and peace seems like nothing more than a luxurious figment of the imagination.*
>
> Luci Swindoll

like papers scattered all over my desk. I don't like leaves scattered on my sidewalk. I prefer to have all my ducks in a row—organized, neat, tidy, and predictable. But there are times when I really wish I could let go a little. I attended one of my mother's art classes once—beginner's watercolor. We were supposed to make a window with flowering vines climbing up and over it. Mom kept urging her students to loosen up: "let the paint flow," and "just see what happens." I thought I was doing just fine, scattering roses on my nearly finished painting. Then, my mom looked over my shoulder and laughed. I had "scattered" roses very precisely—neatly and equally placed in a pattern nature would never have produced.

Our moods and emotions easily become scattered. They're rarely lined up like ducks in a row. We can't get them to stay organized, neat, tidy, or predictable. They can sneak up on us, and turn our day upside down!

1. When our circumstances overwhelm us, our feelings often scatter to the winds. What kinds of emotions did the psalmist experience in these verses?

- Why does David want to give up, according to Psalm 38:10?

- What three words does David use to describe his feelings in Psalm 55:5?

- Without the strength of the LORD, what will happen to our hearts, according to Psalm 73:26?

2. How did Job describe his heart's response to the troubles he was facing in Job 30:27?

3. How does David express the feelings in his heart in Psalm 38:8?

> *I tend to bloom best on sunny days. What has helped me to grow the most through blustery seasons is adjusting my mental attitude.*
> *Mind-checks are a must for me so I don't slide back into unhealthy habits.*
>
> Patsy Clairmont

4. We probably don't use the term "scattered" too often when we're talking about our emotions, but we frequently use the word "overwhelmed." David said, "My spirit was overwhelmed within me" (Ps. 142:3). Why was he on the verge of losing heart, according to Psalm 40:12?

*P*ulled in too many different directions, we barely have time to think. Our schedules are packed. Our fingers are in too many pies. We are spread too thin. We're running in circles. Life becomes a flurry of activity, a rat race, and all hustle and bustle with no moment to catch a breath. The sheer number of our responsibilities is oppressive. We are overactive, over–committed, over-whelmed. Scattered times are times of emotional turmoil. We become scattered when our emotions prevent us from moving forward. We give a dab here and a dab there, but without a concerted effort, we don't make any headway. At times like this, we are easily confused, easily distracted, easily led astray.

> *Years ago I realized that, if I didn't net my flyaway thoughts, I would accomplish very little, learn less, and lead a very disconnected lifestyle. My longing then was to become mentally focused, emotionally balanced, and spiritually fit. Those goals remain at the top of my list, but quite honestly, some seasons I do better than others.*
>
> Patsy Clairmont

5. So where do we turn when these feelings overwhelm us? David knew just where to go. Take a look at the introduction to Psalm 102. How was the writer feeling at that moment? What does Psalm 102:1 say David did when he felt like this?

6. Take a look at Psalm 61:2. Do we need to patch ourselves up before turning to God? What does David ask God to do for him?

7. What is the psalmist's prayer in Psalm 86:11? How does this attitude guard against being scattered?

8. In order to avoid being scattered, our hearts must stay focused—have a purpose. What does David say his heart is doing in Psalm 84:5?

> *When I began to go to Bible classes, for the first time I began to understand numerous benefits that were mine simply because I had put my faith in Jesus Christ. I could actually learn and apply these facts in my daily life, in a way that really made a difference. I didn't have to be knocked down by every wind that blew across my emotional path because I had a fortress and buffer in God's Word.*
>
> Luci Swindoll

✦ DIGGING DEEPER ✦

The busyness of our days is enough to scatter our hearts and leave us overwhelmed. It takes a measure of determination to keep our eyes steadily on our Savior and the path He has set before us. We should join David in saying, "My heart is steadfast, O God, my heart is steadfast" (Ps. 57:7). Let's look at a few more verses that speak of steadfastness:

- Psalm 51:10
- 1 Corinthians 15:58
- Hebrews 3:14

- Psalm 112:7
- Colossians 1:23
- Hebrews 6:19

✦ PONDER & PRAY ✦

We cannot allow the scattering of our emotions to overwhelm us. Join with David this week in praying for the LORD to lead you to the rock. Ask him to unite your heart, instead of letting its moods scatter you to the four winds. Pray for an understanding of God's purpose for your life, so that you can set your heart on a pilgrimage, purposefully moving forward in your spiritual journey.

Want to lift your spirits from the hustle and bustle of the day? Sing to the LORD. When the praises go up, blessings come down. Now isn't that something to sing about?

Thelma Wells

✦ Trinkets to Treasure ✦

The busyness of our days and the deceitfulness of our hearts work against us, but God offers to help us keep our ducks in a row. So, this week's trinket is a rubber duckie! When you are overwhelmed, God offers you a place of peace and safety. Run to Him. Follow Him. And make Him your destination when you set your heart on pilgrimage!

✦ Notes & Prayer Requests ✦

_____

_____

_____

_____

_____

_____

_____

_____

✦ Notes & Prayer Requests ✦

Mary, Mary, Quite Contrary

"Perverse minds are always cooking up something nasty, always stirring up trouble."

Proverbs 6:14 MSG

erversity is not a term we often use nowadays. It's one of those obscure "Bible words" that has fallen out of everyday use since the 1600's. The dictionary defines perversity as "marked by a disposition to oppose or contradict," "obstinately persisting in an error or fault," "wrongly self–willed or stubborn," "capricious, and reluctant to obey." Other synonyms for perverse would be wayward, ungovernable, obstinate, contradictory, and even cranky and peevish. Contrary is another little–used word. It's probably most famous for its inclusion in the nursery rhyme, "Mary, Mary, quite contrary, how does you garden grow?" Definition anyone? "Opposed, contradictory, inconsistent, resistant to guidance or

Which of the Seven Dwarves would you be — Happy, Sleepy, Sneezy, Bashful, Grumpy, Dopey, or Doc?

discipline." Other synonyms for contrary would be headstrong, noncon-formist, rebellious, and ornery. Now, let's apply these two very useful terms to ourselves.

When you were a child, what was the fastest way to get you to do something? The tongue–in–cheek answer to that question—to forbid you to do it. Our perversity is so ingrained in our hearts that even when we are little, we rebel against authority. It's the contrary streak that asks, "Why not?" and "I wonder what'll happen if I do?" How do we show our contrary hearts when we're grown? When we're reluctant to do what we know is right. When we shut our ears to the prompting of the Spirit. When we avoid the direction of the Scriptures. When we act rebelliously, independently, and self–sufficiently. And when we get into a foul mood and sit there, even though we know we shouldn't. In other words, when we act grouchy, surly, grumpy, and just plain cranky.

1. Sometimes, when we run across a verse of Scripture that convicts us, we dig in our heels and resist the change we know needs to come. Our contrary heart puffs itself up and shakes its fist and shouts, "No way!" "Not on your life!" "When pigs fly!" How does Proverbs 19:3 charac-terize such a person?

2. Solomon talks a good deal about perversity in our hearts. In the Book of Proverbs, he is warning his son to guard against it. What does Proverbs 6:14 say is the result of a perverse heart?

3. What else will come of a person with perversity in their heart, according to Proverbs 12:8?

4. Even more striking, what does Proverbs 11:20 say about those who are hiding perversity in their hearts?

A Journal Entry from Luci Swindoll:

April 11, 2000: Today I decided I am really cranky. Without meaning to or wanting to, I'm becoming a cranky, irritable old woman. I hate that and am committed to working on it. It's driving me crazy and is maddening to everybody else. LORD, help me!

*D*o you know someone who is very contrary? The minute someone tells them they have to do something, they don't want to do it. They hate to be told what they'll like, what they'll feel, or what they really ought to try. They go out of their way to be different from other people. They ignore people's suggestions or recommendations, preferring to come up with their own ideas and make up their own mind about things. I know someone like that—Me! And what's sad is I find it easy to excuse this flaw in my nature by pretending it's some kind of enviable character quality—calling it creativity or independence or self–sufficiency. In truth, I am rebellious and proud, contrary and perverse.

Have you ever tried to justify some little deceitfulness in your heart by calling it something else? When God calls us to look into our hearts with honest eyes, we might just find something we didn't want to see. We cannot then ignore it or re–define it. Confess it, and let God help you overcome it.

5. What is the reality of living contrary to God, and what is the result of clinging to our rebellious ways? Take a look at Isaiah's warning:

> *This perverse way of life will be like a towering, badly built wall that slowly, slowly tilts and shifts, and then one day, without warning, collapses.* –Isaiah 30:13 MSG

When you tell the truth, it sets you free. So I made my decision to stop pretending. I gave up. I let go. I stopped being in charge of my spiritual goodness, because I didn't have any spiritual goodness. I had worked for God and yet withheld my heart from Him.

Nicole Johnson

6. What is the consequence of an unrepentant heart, according to Romans 2:5?

7. Look at Jeremiah's prayer of confession in Lamentations 1:20. Why has he been so troubled?

> LORD, *help me not to look for an easy way out. Help me to take responsibility before You and others for my actions and reactions. Thank You that I can choose to give up my childishness and instead experience childlike joy.*
>
> Patsy Clairmont

8. Instead of clinging to our rebellious ways, we are urged to yield to God. Take a look at these Scriptures. What were people who trusted God willing to do?

___ Esther 4:16	a. willing to yield to others
___ Psalm 51:12	b. willing to obey God
___ Matthew 11:15	c. willing to endure
___ 2 Timothy 2:10	d. willing to suffer for Christ
___ James 2:2	e. willing to die
___ James 3:17	f. willing to hear
___ 1 Peter 4:1	g. willing to whatever God told them

9. King Hezekiah's prayer for the people of God was, "Do not be stubborn…but submit yourselves to the LORD" (2 Chr. 30:8 NLT). How does Hebrews 12:9 say we should submit ourselves to God? Why?

✦ DIGGING DEEPER ✦

Most of the time cheerful submission seems like an oxy-moron. How could those two words possibly go together? We tend to think of submission as grudging, not a matter for rejoicing. But God knows our hearts, so when He calls us to obedience, He wants our heart to be in it. God desires cheerful submission. Take a look at these other Scriptures that talk about cheer:

- Matthew 9:2
- John 16:33
- James 5:13
- Matthew 9:22
- 2 Corinthians 9:7

✦ PONDER & PRAY ✦

Has a contrary heart found you resisting what you know to be good and right and true? Does your quiet rebellion leave you feeling cranky and defensive with those around you? Pray this week for the courage to let go, to trust God, to be willing. Pray for joy, so your submission will be cheerful. Pray for a teachable heart, that will not buck against wise counsel. Trust that God's way is the best, and will not crumble and fall like the castles in the air we build for ourselves.

Owning my edginess instead of justifying reactive behavior has helped to improve my disposition.

Patsy Clairmont

✦ TRINKETS TO TREASURE ✦

There's a part of our heart that rebels against God. It's contrary and perverse. It's that little voice whispering, "I don't wanna," and stamps its foot and pouts. And when we find the LORD asking us to do something, it's the part that wants to dig in its heels and shout, "When pigs fly!" So to remind us to guard against our contrary nature, we have a little pig for our trinket this week. God is in the business of miracles, so we should thank Him that the miracle He chooses to make in our lives is not that of a flying pig, but of a changed heart.

✦ NOTES & PRAYER REQUESTS ✦

_____

_____

_____

_____

_____

_____

_____

✦ Notes & Prayer Requests ✦

CHAPTER 10

P.M.S.ING

"IF YOU FALL TO PIECES IN A CRISIS, THERE WASN'T MUCH TO YOU IN THE FIRST PLACE."

Proverbs 24:10 MSG

There's no use trying to deny it. There is an ebb and flow to our moods that corresponds to the female cycle. What's funny is that even though our moods tend to swing at the same pace every month, many of us never realize it's happening! We're too close to it—actually, we're in the middle of it. From our perspective, the boss is just a bit more bossy, the kids are just a bit more quarrelsome, traffic is just a bit more congested, your friends are just a bit more exasperating, and everyone in general has become very irritating. But in truth, they haven't changed at all—we have!

For most of us, when "that time of the month" draws near, we get edgy, touchy, irritable, fractious, annoyed, bad-tempered, moody, sharp-tongued, and downright

CLEARING
✦ THE ✦
COBWEBS

What cues does your body send to let you know where you are in your cycle— increased appetite, cheerfulness, quietness, paranoia, depression, cravings, exhaustion?

grumpy. We're on a short fuse, and people walk around us as if they're treading on eggshells. Other women face the onset of their period with a different demeanor. They become quiet, introspective, super–sensitive, and weepy. They feel guilty for things they didn't do or are hard on them-selves for things they did do. It would all be so hilarious if it weren't so true.

This Jekyll–Hyde transformation we go through each month isn't really inexplicable. We're not changed. We just reveal what's in our hearts with fewer inhibitions!

> *There are days when I start feeling blue. On those days I've learned to avoid certain things. I won't weigh myself, listen to sad music, get a haircut, open a box of chocolates, or shop for a bathing suit.*
>
> Barbara Johnson

1. We often hear how people reveal their true character when placed in a crisis situation. When pressed, our strengths and weaknesses are thrust into the spotlight. Take a look at this verse in James:

You know that under pressure, your faith–life is forced into the open and shows its true colors. —James 1:3 MSG

*W*hen you undergo premenstrual pressures, how does your faith hold up?

2. Solomon said, "People eventually reveal by their actions if their motives are on the up and up" (Prov. 20:11 MSG). What is revealed by our hearts, according to Proverbs 27:19?

3. God has always told us He knows what's in our hearts. Jesus was never fooled by people who were outwardly righteous. What does He condemn people of in Matthew 15:8?

> *If my mind becomes cluttered by the day's annoyances, it's a given that sooner or later I'm going to lose my self control. If I lose my self–control, for sure I'm going to lose my joy. I hate losing my joy. Fortunately, I have a choice in how I react.*
>
> Marilyn Meberg

4. Jesus said, "those things which proceed out of the mouth come from the heart" (Matt. 15:18). Our words reveal what we hide inside. What is revealed by our words, according to Matthew 12:34, 35?

5. Peter's first epistle tells us the "hidden person of the heart" is where the LORD's eyes are fixed (1 Pet. 3:4). He is in the business of changing us from the inside out. Only He can give us the new heart we need. He offers it to us:

> *I'll give you a new heart, put a new spirit in you. I'll remove the stone heart from your body and replace it with a heart that's God–willed, not self–willed.* —Ezekiel 36:26 MSG

*W*hat's the difference between a heart that is God–willed and one that is self–willed?

6. What did Paul want to be revealed in his life, according to the first part of Galatians 1:16?

> *Choosing to let go of my tempestuous responses is making a huge difference in my life. I want to be the fragrance of Christ in the midst of the storms of life, not part of the storm front.*
>
> Sheila Walsh

*I*t's silly to pretend we're always skipping along under blue skies with a happy heart. There are days when we just don't feel like skipping. There are days when the skies are not blue, but a nondescript shade of beige. We feel blah. Lackluster. Uninspired. Disinterested. We just don't care. Those are the days when we're not in the mood for anything. We don't feel like smiling. We don't feel like talking. We don't feel like working. We don't feel like cooking. And we certainly don't feel like putting any effort into being pleasant. Often, we'd really rather everyone just go away. Unfortunately, we cannot pause life just because we're not in the mood for it. A woman's got to do what a woman's got to do, whether she feels like it or not. Those are times when we have to reach right down into that new heart of ours and find enough strength from the LORD to make it through the next day, the next hour, or even the next minute.

7. When you see a woman who is clearly "not in the mood" at that moment, give her some space! What does the very wise and experienced King Solomon say about being a little too sweet and cheerful to someone who'd rather not endure you just now? It's in Proverbs 25:20.

> *One of the greatest tests of character is to be loving and gracious when we'd rather not. When Scripture tells us "a friend loves at all times," we may want that, but the ability to do it has to come from the* LORD.
>
> Luci Swindoll

8. Moods, cycles, and P.M.S. are all part of being a woman. It's a hurdle we can't avoid, so we may as well face it head on. Women have struggled with these things for centuries, as evidenced in some of the things Solomon says about women. What words does he use to describe women? Can you find yourself in any of these proverbs?

- *Foolishness is like a loud woman; she does not have wisdom or knowledge.* —Proverbs 9:13 NCV

- *As a ring of gold in a swine's snout, So is a lovely woman who lacks discretion.* —Proverbs 11:22

- *A wise woman strengthens her family, but a foolish woman destroys hers by what she does.* —Proverbs 14:1 NCV

- *Better to live alone in a tumbledown shack than share a mansion with a nagging spouse.* —Proverbs 21:9 MSG

> • *It is better to live alone in the desert than with a quarreling and complaining wife.* —Proverbs 21:19 NCV

> *I realize how tart I become when inconvenienced. It doesn't take much of a breeze to topple me. I want to believe that, if called upon to be a heroine, I would rise to the occasion. But experience has proven me feeble.*
>
> Patsy Clairmont

> • *It is better to live alone in the corner of an attic than with a contentious wife in a lovely home.* —Proverbs 25:24 NLT

> • *A nagging spouse is like the drip, drip, drip of a leaky faucet.* —Proverbs 27:15 MSG

9. When we're tempted to start P.M.S.ing, we need to be wise. King Solomon says the beginning of wisdom is the fear of the LORD. And "a woman who fears the LORD, she shall be praised" (Prov. 31:30). How do we fear God? Let's match the verse with its text in these verses about the fear of the LORD. Each one couples the fear in our heart with the action inspired by it.

___ Deuteronomy 6:2	a. Fear the LORD and love Him.
___ Deuteronomy 8:6	b. Fear the LORD and do not rebel.
___ Deuteronomy 10:12	c. Fear the LORD and depart from evil.
___ Deuteronomy 10:20	d. Fear the LORD and keep His commandments.
___ Joshua 24:14	e. Fear the LORD and trust Him.
___ 1 Samuel 12:14	f. Fear the LORD and hold fast to Him.
___ 1 Samuel 12:24	g. Fear the LORD and find know edge of Him.

___ Psalm 22:23

___ Psalm 33:8

___ Psalm 115:11

___ Psalm 135:20

___ Proverbs 2:5

___ Proverbs 3:7
___ Proverbs 19:23

h. Fear the LORD and serve Him in sincerity, truth.

i. Fear the LORD and serve Him with all your heart.

j. Fear the LORD and walk in His ways.

k. Fear the LORD and live a satisfied life.

l. Fear the LORD and stand in awe of Him.

m. Fear the LORD and bless Him.

n. Fear the LORD and praise Him.

✦ DIGGING DEEPER ✦

When we live a life characterized by the fear of the LORD, even the emotional ebb and flow of the month will not completely shake us from our firm footing in His Word. Instead, the LORD we serve will characterize our lives. We who serve Jesus will become like Him, and others will see Christ in us. Here are a few verses that talk about Christ in us:

- 2 Corinthians 11:10
- Galatians 2:20
- 2 Corinthians 13:3
- 1 Timothy 1:16

✦ PONDER & PRAY ✦

Sometimes we need to be reminded of the seriousness with which God deals with sin. He doesn't accept excuses, even on P.M.S. days. Remember the words of Isaiah: "The LORD of hosts, Him you shall hallow; Let Him be your fear, And let him be your dread" (Is. 8:13). Ask the LORD to help you understand His holiness this week. Ask Him to teach your heart the godly fear that will lead to life. Then pray for the strength to become a woman who fears the LORD, not a foolish woman who is ruled by her moods.

✦ TRINKETS TO TREASURE ✦

Are you familiar with the phrase "stepping on eggshells"? If people are stepping on eggshells around you, it means they're tip–toeing around you, quiet as a mouse, hoping not to do anything to disturb or upset you. They think you're volatile, unpredictable, apt to explode, and they aren't sure what might set you off. This week's trinket is an eggshell—one that's been blown out, so it's light and fragile. When the urge to start P.M.S.ing hits you each month, keep in mind that our goal should not be to have people treading lightly in fear of us, but we should be walking in the fear of the LORD.

✦ Notes & Prayer Requests ✦

✦ Notes & Prayer Requests ✦

CHAPTER 11

MIXED–UP EMOTIONS

"EVEN IN LAUGHTER THE HEART MAY SORROW, AND THE END OF MIRTH MAY BE GRIEF."

Proverbs 14:13

We've probably all had our share of scares and adventures behind the wheel of a car. Turning the wrong way onto a one–way street. Bumping up over a curb so we're parked with one wheel on the sidewalk. Scraping the paint off our license plate when we pull too far into a parking spot. Digs, dents, scrapes, scratches, flat tires, and fender benders. But even without the little mishaps, just navigating on unfamiliar roads can be more of an adventure than we bargained for. Trying to gauge which direction you're pointed when the road keeps curving. Are we still headed east? Unraveling a tangled freeway system.

CLEARING + THE + COBWEBS

Do you navigate by landmark, or by street sign?

Which leaf of the cloverleaf? Getting turned around. Having to back-track. Losing ourselves along the way.

Mixed up emotions are like mixed up directions. We're trying to navigate life's highways, but we have feelings pulling us in different directions. We zip along, chasing after other peoples' expectations of us. We detour around situations that might make us feel guilty or uncomfortable. We watch for pleasant diversions—doughnut shops, ice cream parlors, shoe sales. And distracted by all the things that catch our eyes and tug at our hearts, we meander aimlessly through side streets and back alleys. We're unsure which way we should have been going in the first place. We've become lost. We're confused. We've gone astray.

Surrendering our agenda for our lives is the hardest thing we will do. I wish for you the willingness to look right at the hidden parts of yourself and allow honest exposure and confession to take place.

Nicole Johnson

1. Women are quite capable of emotional multi–tasking. When we find ourselves with mixed emotions, we can become flustered by them—confused. Which feeling is the right one? When our heart tugs us in two different direc-tions, what does Paul remind us in Ephesians 4:17–24?

2. Proverbs 9:16 asks, "Are you confused about life, don't know what's going on?" (MSG). How did Jesus respond to the crowds that followed Him, according to Matthew 9:36?

3. God often refers to us as little lost sheep. He knows how much we need His guidance. How do the following verses describe our lives as lambs?

- Why does Isaiah 53:6 say we've lost our way?

- How does Jeremiah 23:4 describe the life of a sheep without a shepherd?

- What do lost sheep do, according to Jeremiah 50:6?

4. What is the cry of the lost sheep, according to Psalm 119:176?

5. When we feel turned around and confused by the clamoring of our moods and emotions, it's important to remember God won't leave us lost. Isaiah scolded the Jews, saying, "Why would you ever complain…saying, 'God has lost track of me. He doesn't care what happens to me'?" (Is. 40:27 MSG). What is God's provision for the lost, according to Luke 19:10?

> *I have great empathy for those who struggle with erratic emotions because I know how overwhelming unpredictable emotions can be, feelings that flood in with such force they affect even your physical well-being. In my emotionally chaotic years, I had more symptoms than a dog has fleas.*
>
> Patsy Clairmont

*O*ur emotions are capable of an amazing progression. Early in our marriage, my husband headed out for an evening meeting. Sure he'd be home at any time, I sat up waiting for him. Hour after hour passed, and still no sound of the key in the door. While I paced restlessly through our home, my mood underwent some incredible shifts. At first, I was just mildly concerned— "The meeting must have run late." Then I began to have real worries— "Car trouble?" Pretty soon I was worried sick— "An accident? Sudden illness?" Before long, I was planning what to wear to his funeral. Then, I started to get upset— "Why didn't he call?" Upset crossed over into blistering fury and resentment— "How could he do this to me?" And when he finally pulled in, there were tears of relief and emotional exhaustion. Have you ever ridden that emotional roller coaster?

> *I'm not denigrating the feelings and desires that cross our minds. Feelings aren't what do us in, though they constantly demand satisfaction. We are done in when we live out of these ever changing—feelings.*
>
> Luci Swindoll

6. What does God say He will do in Ezekiel 34:16?

7. God knew that we need a shepherd. Left to our own whims, we would only stray into trouble. "You were lost sheep with no idea who you were or where you were going. Now you're named and kept for good by the Shepherd of your souls" (1 Pet. 2:25 MSG). Look at these verses about our Good Shepherd:

___ Isaiah 40:11   a. He knows His sheep, and they know Him.

___ John 10:11   b. He will lead us to living fountains.

___ John 10:14   c. He gently leads those of us with young.

___ Hebrews 13:20   d. He is coming again for us.

___ 1 Peter 5:4   e. He gives His life for the sheep.

___ Revelation 7:17 f. He is the Great Shepherd of the sheep.

8. Our Shepherd will lead us onto the right path. He knows the way we should go. All we have to do is follow Him.

- What is the danger of going it alone, according to Proverbs 14:12?

- How shall we know we're on the right path, according to Isaiah 30:21?

- What has been prepared for us, according to Isaiah 35:8?

9. No matter how mixed–up we might become, God is there to lead us along when we seek Him. The psalms are filled with prayers asking God to take charge. When we surrender the controls to Him, we can be sure He will lead us on the right paths.

___ Psalm 5:8	a. Lead me and guide me.
___ Psalm 25:5	b. Lead me and hold me in Your hand.
___ Psalm 31:3	c. Lead me in Your righteousness.
___ Psalm 43:3	d. Lead me in the land of uprightness.
___ Psalm 139:10	e. Lead me in Your truth and teach me.
___ Psalm 139:24	f. Lead me by Your light and Your truth.
___ Psalm 143:10	g. Lead me in the way everlasting.

✦ DIGGING DEEPER ✦

God's way is a good way, and we can entrust our lives to His leading and care. Take a look at some more verses about the paths in which the LORD leads us.

- Psalm 16:11
- Psalm 18:36
- Psalm 119:35
- Psalm 119:105
- Proverbs 4:26

✦ PONDER & PRAY ✦

This week you can talk to the LORD as a sheep to your Shepherd. Tell Him your concerns and confusion. Let Him know what's been on your mind lately. Ask Him for the strength, comfort, nourishment, and peace only He can provide. Just don't ask Him where He's going to take you. Trust that part in His hands, and follow Him fearlessly. His is a good path.

✦ TRINKETS TO TREASURE ✦

Mixed–up moods and emotions can be our downfall some days. They leave us feeling muddled and uncertain about what to do next. Pulled in too many different directions, we don't end up going anywhere! This week's little gift will be a whisk. Whenever you're scrambling eggs, you can think of your scrambled thoughts and feelings. Just remember, when you're feeling lost, don't rush around in a panic. Just call out to the Shepherd of your soul, and He will lead you back onto the right path.

Years of childish actions passed before I realized how selfish and destructive my moody behavior was. It wasn't easy to break my old response patterns, but it was liberating. I gradually learned not to give into swings in my emotions but to give up my need to be in control.

Patsy Clairmont

✦ Notes & Prayer Requests ✦

CHAPTER 12

KNOW THYSELF!

"HELP ME UNDERSTAND, SO I CAN KEEP YOUR TEACHINGS, OBEYING THEM WITH ALL MY HEART."

Psalm 119:34 NCV

Some days, our feelings seem out of control. We're just reacting to everything that lands in front of us, and we feel like we just can't help it. Emotions are often compared to a roller coaster—dizzying heights, plunging depths, and unexpected turns. And moods are said to swing like a pendulum, from one extreme to another. Like it or not, a woman's heart is often just one big bundle of emotions, so it's absolutely vital to take the time to sort through all those emotions and try to understand them. Solomon calls our heart the "wellspring of life" (Prov. 4:23). It's the starting point of who we are, and it determines who we will become. That's why it's so important to guard your heart! Solomon urges us to "Keep your heart with all diligence." And a part of the

CLEARING ✦ THE ✦ COBWEBS

Why is it easier to understand others than it is to understand yourself?

keeping is paying attention to what's going on in there. We need to get to know ourselves, understand what's going on inside, be in touch with our emotions, know what makes us tick. God has given us all these emotions, and it's our job to be good stewards of them.

Stewardship is something we talk a lot about in church. We need to be good stewards of our money, good stewards of our time, good stewards of our gifts. Do you know where the word "steward" comes from? It's one of those words that has changed slightly over time. It's an old English word. The "ward" part means someone in charge of something, kind of like a keeper or warden. The "ste" part was originally sty. So there you have it. Steward comes from sty–ward, or keeper of the pigsty. I think it's very appropriate to remember that we must be good stewards of our moods and emotions, because sometimes they can be in such a state, it seems like a pigsty!

As we consider our established patterns in life, confront the unknown, and dig inside ourselves for courage and resources, something new will gradually emerge. We will change. We will gain a perspective that touches every part of our beings, and it will bring to life in us latent and unrealized capabilities and dreams that are ours simply because we are alive.

Luci Swindoll

1. Mood management can only come through careful stewardship. Scripture says we can only learn to discern good from evil if we have exercised our senses to do so (Heb. 5:14). Since we know good from evil, what's the best thing we can do, according to Ecclesiastes 3:12?

2. When faced with a dilemma, Jesus urged people to use righteous judgment in deciding what to do. "Use your head—and heart!—to discern what is right, to test what is authentically right" (John 7:24 MSG). We all face choices, and we must take care in the choosing. What was Joshua's choice in Joshua 24:15?

> *Surrendering to God is the key that unlocks the door to the life you want. A bigger spiritual "to do" list or a calendar full of church activities will not change our lives. When we give ourselves to God—mind, body, soul, and spirit—He changes us.*
>
> Nicole Johnson

3. Doing the right thing may seem like a no–brainer, but when it comes down to the nitty–gritty of living, being good can be very hard! That's where careful stewardship needs to meet supernatural assistance. What does Psalm 105:4 say we should do?

4. What did Paul depend on, according to Colossians 1:29?

5. Of course, depending on God doesn't magically make our moods fall into line. That's not what Paul was saying at all. In fact, this same verse, as translated in *The Message*, gives us a better idea of how hard it is to depend on God. "That's what I'm working so hard at day after day, year after year, doing my best with the energy God so generously gives me." Match up these other verses that speak about dependence.

___ Deuteronomy 7:9   a. We can depend on God's strength (MSG).

___ Psalm 33:20   b. Depend on God in whatever you do (NCV).

___ Psalm 147:11   c. God is a God you can depend on (MSG).

___ Proverbs 3:7   d. Depend on God and receive peace (NCV).

___ Proverbs 16:3   e. We depend on the LORD alone to save us (NLT).

___ Isaiah 26:3   f. We cannot depend on our own wisdom (NCV).

6. So, why did God give us these muddling emotions anyhow? Is it just one of those "great things which we cannot comprehend" (Job 37:5)? What wouldn't we be able to comprehend if we didn't have these emotions, according to Ephesians 3:17–19?

After everything we've talked about so far, it might seem as if our moods and emotions are a curse rather than a blessing. They give us so much trouble! What good are moods if they only make us crazy? What good are emotions if they only confuse us? But God has given women all these emotions for a very good reason. Think about it. Women are much more empathetic. We are able to put ourselves in another's place and understand instinctively how someone else is feeling. We cry easily because we feel for one another. Women are capable of great understanding, great compassion, and great mercy. When Jesus urged His followers to love one another, care for one another, and encourage one another, He gave women a commission for which they were perfectly suited!

7. Emotions are gifts from God, but that doesn't mean we will automatically use them as we should. Just look at Paul—he battled with himself all the time. We will too. What was Peter's encouragement to those with gifts in 1 Peter 4:10?

> *The things we fear (pain, failure, disgrace, rejection, limitations) are ultimately some of our finest teachers, educating us in compassion, grace, wisdom, and understanding.*
>
> Patsy Clairmont

8. Over and over, we are encouraged to trust God and do good. Our moods often hamper us, but at some point, we need to step out in faith and "just do it."

- What does Isaiah 1:17 say about doing good?

- Whom should we be doing good things for, according to Galatians 6:10?

- What pleases God, according to Hebrews 13:16?

I prize those qualities within us women—our interest in relationships at deep levels and our ability to nudge, encourage, and promote well-being. In fact, I just love being a woman. I am complex; at times I am a contradiction, occasionally I am a cacophony of emotions.

Patsy Clairmont

9. Doing good will prove to be a lifelong battle for us. We may gain great wisdom. We may show great faith. We may bear much fruit. But we'll never "arrive" here on this earth. Our guard will always have to be up, and our dependence on God must be complete. Sound like a long, exhausting fight? Paul knew it might seem so. What encouragement does he offer to all believers in Galatians 6:9?

✦ DIGGING DEEPER ✦

When we depend on Christ for what we need, the Bible assures us that we can overcome anything—even mood swings and unmanageable emotions! Take a look at just a few verses about overcoming:

- John 16:33
- 1 John 4:4
- Romans 12:21
- 1 John 5:4

✦ PONDER & PRAY ✦

As we close this study, pray that God will bring back to your mind all the lessons you have needed to hear. Pray especially for the discernment to know yourself and the determination to do good each and every day. Ask the LORD to show you all the ways He is faithful, and thereby strengthen your faith. Put your trust in Him, and depend on Him for help with your heart—the moods, emotions, and feelings He has given you to use for the good of others and for His glory.

✦ TRINKETS TO TREASURE ✦

Your trinket this week is a little tiny chair—like the kind you see in a dollhouse. While you work through what is right and doing good, this little chair will be your reminder to depend on God through it all. A chair is the perfect picture of faith in action. You don't give it a thought when you sit in a chair—you just expect it to hold you up. You might say you trust God to hold you up, but until you place yourself in His hands, they are just words. May your complete dependence on God's strength come as naturally as sitting down on a chair.

✦ NOTES & PRAYER REQUESTS ✦

✦ SHALL WE REVIEW? ✦

Every chapter has added a new trinket to your treasure trove of memories. Let's remind ourselves of the lessons they hold for us!

1. A rubber band ball.

This little reminder about the complexity of our hearts shows just how intertwined our moods and emotions can be. It doesn't take very much to leave us with a tangled mess!

2. Soap.

Our heart is deceitful, and as slippery as wet soap. If we keep this in mind, we can be on guard against the whims of emotion. When we are wise, we cannot be led astray by the wiles of the heart.

3. A firecracker.

A small reminder to watch our temper, because it can be a dangerous. little thing. When we do and say things in the heat of the moment, a lot of damage can occur.

4. Grass seed.

At times, it might seem that the grass is greener in someone else's lawn, but we must guard our hearts against jealousy. We must remember we are accountable to God for our own lives, and for how well the seeds He's planted in us have flourished.

5. A braided cord.

When our hearts are lonely, we realize how much the bonds of friendship mean. And when we have no other friends, how much more tightly we must weave our lives together with Jesus'! He is a Friend who can lift our hearts out of loneliness, for He knows us and loves us and encourages us to cultivate a friendship with Him.

6. A butterfly.

This trinket helps us to remember that when we get butterflies in our stomachs, we must trust God to take care of us.

7. A watering can.

It is so important to keep our heart fed and watered. Otherwise the doldrums of life can roll in, drying us out and leaving us thirsty.

8. A rubber duckie.

This is a reminder that God can help us get our ducks back in a row when circumstances work to scatter our thoughts and feelings.

9. A pig.

Our contrary nature likes to rebel against what is good. In our hearts, we resist God, and shout, "I don't wanna," and "When pigs fly!" When God performs a miracle in our lives, it isn't to give the pig some wings, but to give us a new heart.

10. An eggshell.

When "that time of the month" descends, our trinket reminds us that people should not have to walk on eggshells around us. They won't have to tread lightly around us because we'll be walking in the fear of the LORD.

11. A whisk.

Our emotions mix us up and lead us astray. Our trinket is a little reminder of how our feelings are muddled up like a scrambled egg, and all we need to do is call out to the Shepherd of our soul.

12. A chair.

We must get to know ourselves, and we need to discern what is right and good. But when it comes right down to it, we need to depend upon God with the same faith we show when we sit down on a chair. We must place ourselves in His hands and trust Him to hold us up.

✦ LEADER'S GUIDE ✦

Chapter 1

1. e, c, a, f, d, h, b, g.

2. "A merry heart makes a cheerful countenance, But by sorrow of the heart the spirit is broken" (Prov. 15:13). Cheerfulness and a merry heart on the one hand, sorrow on the other.

3. "A man's heart plans his way, But the LORD directs his steps" (Prov. 16:9). Our hearts are filled with everything that makes us...us! Our feelings, our dreams, our commitments, our loyalties, our personality, and our plans. It's such a busy place, it's no wonder we find ourselves in so much turmoil!

4. "The troubles of my heart have enlarged; Bring me out of my distresses" (Ps. 25:17). Often, when we're in distress, our troubles seem to enlarge. They take on huge proportions and soon they fill our minds. "If I regard iniquity in my heart, the LORD will not hear" (Ps. 66:18). If we harbor unconfessed sin in our hearts, God will not hear our prayers. As one translation puts it, "If I had been cozy with evil, the LORD would never have listened" (MSG). "I am poor and needy, And my heart is wounded within me" (Ps. 109:22). Only God can heal a wounded heart. David was right in turning to the LORD with his.

5. "My heart is stricken and withered like grass, so that I forget to eat my bread" (Ps. 102:4). When our hearts are overwhelmed with troubles, we often lose our appetites.

6. "For out of much affliction and anguish of heart I wrote to you, with many tears, not that you should be grieved, but that you might know the love which I have so abundantly for you" (2 Cor. 2:4). Paul tells his friends in Corinth how he has felt affliction and anguish in his heart. He has shed tears over them, worried about their reaction, and wants very badly for the recipients of the letter to know how much he loves them.

7. "He who doubts is like a wave of the sea, driven and tossed by the wind" (James 1:6). This isn't the only time this imagery is used to describe a person led along by the emotion of the moment. Paul compares those people who don't use their minds concerning the faith to children, "tossed to and fro and carried about with every wind of doctrine, by the trickery of men, in the cunning craftiness of deceitful plotting" (Eph. 4:14). When we allow our moods to manage us, instead of the other way around, we are likely to be led along by anyone who can manipulate our feelings!

8. "That is why we have a great High Priest who has gone to heaven, Jesus the Son of God. Let us cling to him and never stop trusting him. This High Priest of ours understands our weaknesses, for he faced all of the same temptations we do, yet he did not sin" (Heb. 4:14, 15 NLT). Jesus knows all about mood swings, cravings, disappointments, and embarrassment. He understands sadness, mixed feelings, misgivings, and relief. The writer of Hebrews says Jesus understands us so well because He went through it all too.

9. "Let the word of Christ dwell in you richly in all wisdom, teaching and admonishing one another in psalms and hymns and spiritual songs, singing with grace in your hearts to the LORD" (Col. 3:16). Don't be ruled by your present mood. Instead, let your heart be ruled by Scripture—the Word of Christ dwelling in you! When we heed Jesus' words, we find ourselves in paths of wisdom. We'll be able to reach out to others who are struggling and tell them what we've learned. We'll be able to encourage one another along the way, and our hearts will be filled with songs of praise and thanksgiving. When Scripture is firmly planted in our hearts, we cannot be manipulated by our moods.

Chapter 2

1. "Take heed to yourselves, lest your heart be deceived, and you turn aside and serve other gods and worship them" (Deut. 11:16). God wants us to be on guard. Our hearts can be deceived, so we must protect them. If we don't take heed, we might be lured away from the right path.

2. "The heart is deceitful above all things, And desperately wicked; Who can know it?" (Jer. 17:9). Selfishness is deeply rooted in our hearts. It dictates our decisions, our first impulses, and our gut reactions. Our hearts are deceitful—easily wooed away from what is right and good. Even after we have given our hearts to God, our hearts can betray us and lead us into sin.

3. "For from within, out of the heart of men, proceed evil thoughts, adulteries, fornications, murders, thefts, covetousness, wickedness, deceit, lewdness, an evil eye, blasphemy, pride, foolishness" (Mark 7:21, 22). Look what sin has done. These are the things that come most naturally to fallen people. As the old saying goes, "But for the grace of God, there go I."

4. "He who trusts in his own heart is a fool, But whoever walks wisely will be delivered" (Prov. 28:26). We are fools if we follow our hearts and our hearts alone. Engage your brain, and you'll be able to walk wisely. You can learn to have a balance between your head and your heart.

5. In 1 Samuel 16:7, the LORD tells Samuel He is not deceived by outward appearances. He looks right into the hearts of men and women. Psalm 44:21 says that God "knows the secrets of the heart." In Jeremiah 17:10, God says, "I, the LORD, search the heart, I test the mind." And best of all, Hebrews 4:12 tells us we have a way to understand ourselves clearly right in our own Bibles. "The word of God is living and powerful, and sharper than any two-edged sword, piercing even to the division of soul and spirit, and of joints and marrow, and is a discerner of the thoughts and intents of the heart." If you are looking for ways to manage your moods, the Scriptures can give you the insight you'll need!

6. "Trust in the LORD with all your heart, and lean not on your own understanding" (Prov. 3:5). God is upfront with us. He tells us outright how we can't trust our emotions. Instead, He pleads with us to put our trust in Him. Take Him at His word. Believe Him, and act on what He asks of us. That's our alternative!

7. "The LORD is near to those who have a broken heart, And saves such as have a contrite spirit" (Ps. 34:18). God is able to help us, but only if we come to Him with brokenness—admitting our inability to help ourselves, confessing our failings, and ready to submit to His guidance.

8. "Create in me a clean heart, O God, And renew a steadfast spirit within me" (Ps. 51:10). God can change our hearts, but we need to ask Him to do it! Even when we have sinned, the Scriptures invite us to "Get rid of all the sins you have done, and get for yourselves a new heart and a new way of thinking" (Ezek. 18:31 NCV). The writer of Hebrews describes the cleansing of our hearts as "having our hearts sprinkled from an evil conscience and our bodies washed with pure water" (Heb. 10:22).

9. "I will give you a new heart and put a new spirit within you; I will take the heart of stone out of your flesh and give you a heart of flesh" (Ezek. 36:26). Even though our hearts are hard, deceitful, and selfish, God is able to give us a new heart. He can give us a heart that longs to follow after Him.

Chapter 3

1. In anger, Moses broke the tablets upon which God had written the Ten Commandments. In frustration, Balaam struck his donkey and threatened to kill it, even though the animal had saved his life. David's older brother accused David of snooping around camp. "I know you are proud and wicked at heart" (1 Sam. 17:38 NCV). Words like that are bitter, presumptuous, and able to wound. In Saul's anger, he shouted at his son Jonathan, "You son of a wicked, worthless woman!" (1 Sam. 20:30 NCV). Ouch! Later, King David's anger was stirred by a story of injustice, and rashly sentenced the perpetrator to death, not realizing he was the guilty party. In Esther, King Ahasuerus was furious by his queen's refusal to appear at his feast. In his anger, he banished her, and then moped over it later because he missed her. And last but not least, there's Jonah. I'm not sure I'd want to be remembered for the childish mood and back–talk we find in Jonah 4:9!

2. "Those who control their anger have great understanding; those with a hasty temper will make mistakes" (Prov. 14:29 NLT). Perhaps the first step in controlling our tempers is the understanding of things that make us erupt. Losing our tempers never does any good. It will always lead us into words and deeds we'll regret later.

3. "An angry man stirs up strife, And a furious man abounds in transgression" (Prov. 29:22). Angry people stir up trouble. Angry people sin bountifully.

4. "Do not hasten in your spirit to be angry, For anger rests in the bosom of fools" (Eccl. 7:9). None of us wants to play the fool.

5. Psalms says "Cease from anger" (Ps. 37:8). Cease. That means, "Stop it!" Ephesians 4:31 says anger should be "Put away from you." Put away. And in Colossians 3:8, Paul says to "put off" anger. *Put off.* Other translations use words like "stop," "turn," "don't," "bridle," "cool your pipes," "make a clean break," "get rid of," "put these things out of your life."

6. We can't pretend we don't get angry. We can't suppress the emotion and deny its existence. We get angry. But the Bible helps us. "Be angry, and do not sin" (Ps. 4:4). There are times when anger is justified. There are times when anger is the right reaction in a situation. But care must be taken in how anger is shown. Don't let your anger lead to sin.

7. "He who is slow to anger is better than the mighty, And he who rules his spirit than he who takes a city" (Prov. 16:32). When you are guarding your heart and managing your moods, you can detect the beginnings of anger. Then, you can search out your motives, watch your reactions, and slow down the rush towards an explosion. With God's help, we won't be at the mercy of a quick temper.

Chapter 4

1. Let's compare translations on this passage. They're all just a little different. "A sound heart is life to the body, But envy is rottenness to the bones" (Prov. 14:30). "A relaxed attitude lengthens life; jealousy rots it away" (NLT). "Peace of mind means a healthy body, but jealousy will rot your bones" (NCV). "A sound mind makes for a robust body, but runaway emotions corrode the bones" (MSG).

2. In Luke 11:39, Jesus is rebuking men who hide their true motives, "Now you Pharisees make the outside of the cup and dish clean, but your inward part is full of greed and wickedness." Our psalms passage talks about slander and gossip. The verse in Proverbs talks about the backbiting tongue—another word for gossip. In 2 Peter, a sinner is said to "have a heart trained in covetous practices."

3. "He who is greedy for gain troubles his own house" (Prov. 15:27). "Woe to him who covets evil gain for his house" (Hab. 2:9). Jealousy, greed, and covetousness only lead to sin.

4. "Incline my heart to Your testimonies, and not to covetousness" (Ps. 119:36). Don't let covetousness dictate your actions. Don't do something just because you're keeping up with the Joneses. Don't adjust your standards to fit the current levels of social acceptability. The psalmist says our hearts should lean towards God's Word, and that should dictate our actions.

5. "Let no one seek his own, but each one the other's well-being" (1 Cor. 10:24). "Let each of you look out not only for his own interests, but also for the interests of others" (Phil. 2:4). The message seems to be, get your eyes off of yourself! We can guard against covetousness by focusing instead on meeting the needs of others.

6. "But Martha was distracted with much serving, and she approached Him and said, 'LORD, do You not care that my sister has left me to serve alone? Therefore tell her to help me'" (Luke 10:40). I'm so glad she asked, because otherwise we might never know what Jesus had to say about the subject! He says, "My dear Martha, you are so upset over all these details! There is really only one thing worth being concerned about. Mary has discovered it—and I won't take it away from her" (Luke

10:41, 42 NLT). Like Martha, we need to look up from all the details we fuss over and study the bigger picture. Otherwise we might miss the whole point!

7. I wonder if Peter was worried about fairness here? For whatever reason, he had his eyes on John. "Peter seeing him, said to Jesus, 'But LORD, what about this man?'" (John 21:21). Jesus didn't miss a beat, and gently put Peter in his place. "What is that to you? You follow Me" (John 21:22 NLT).

8. "Now he who plants and he who waters are one, and each one will receive his own reward according to his own labor" (1 Cor. 3:8). We're all equal in God's eyes. He has no partiality. He plays no favorites. The LORD will be just in rewarding each of us according to our faithfulness, so we shouldn't compare ourselves with others.

9. "Make a careful exploration of who you are and the work you have been given, and then sink yourself into that. Don't be impressed with yourself. Don't compare yourself with others. Each of you must take responsibility for doing the creative best you can with your own life" (Gal. 6:4, 5 MSG). Search out your own heart. Examine your actions. It's between you and the LORD. When you find you have grown and changed, then you will have something to rejoice with the LORD over!

Chapter 5

1. Throughout his travels, Paul experienced many hardships, and not all of them were physical. Even though he had many friends, traveled with several companions, and was close to God, Paul knew loneliness. He knew what it was like to spend sleepless nights, and he knew what it was like to feel lonely. Paul wasn't somehow exempt. Even the "greatest" of Christians has these kinds of feelings. We all do.

2. "Reproach has broken my heart, And I am full of heaviness; I looked for someone to take pity, but there was none; And for comforters, but I found none" (Ps. 69:20). David feels like an outsider, an outcast. He has no one to tell his troubles to. His heart is heavy, and he wants to pour out some of his sorrow. He wants someone to help him bear the load, to comfort him in his sadness, but no one has come alongside.

3. "Two people can accomplish more than twice as much as one; They get a better return for their labor. If one person falls, the other can reach out and help. But people who are alone when they fall are in real trouble. And on a cold night, two under the same blanket can gain warmth from each other. But how can one be warm alone? A person standing alone can be attacked and defeated, but two can stand back–to–back and conquer. Three are even better, for a triple–braided cord is not easily broken" (Eccl. 4:9–12 NLT).

4. "Now she who is really a widow, and left alone, trusts in God and continues in supplications and prayers night and day" (1 Tim. 5:5). Many of us are not widows, but we are single, or we don't have close friends, or we spend many a solitary hour, or it could be the only people we see all day are preschoolers. When there is no one to talk to, we must turn to God. Paul says our option is to trust Him and to pray. When there's no one else to listen, He will.

5. "Trust in Him at all times, you people; Pour out your heart before Him; God is a refuge for us" (Ps. 62:8). You are not left alone. God is your refuge from loneliness, and He welcomes us to pour out our hearts before Him.

6. "Finally, brethren, farewell. Become complete. Be of good comfort, be of one mind, live in peace; and the God of love and peace will be with you" (2 Cor. 13:11). The God of love and peace is with us! Wow!

7. "Now may the LORD of peace Himself give you peace always in every way. The LORD be with you all" (2 Thess. 3:16). "The LORD Jesus Christ be with your spirit. Grace be with you. Amen" (2 Tim. 4:22). Jesus is with us!

8. "And I will pray the Father, and He will give you another Helper, that He may abide with you forever—the Spirit of truth, whom the world cannot receive, because it neither sees Him nor knows Him; but you know Him, for He dwells with you and will be in you" (John 14:16, 17).

9. In 2 Corinthians, Paul says we have "the grace of the LORD Jesus Christ," "the love of God," and "the communion of the Holy Spirit" with us. In Colossians, Paul says he is with his fellow believers in spirit. Isn't it nice to think Paul is rejoicing when we do good and remain steadfast in the faith? And 2 John 1:3 says "Grace, mercy, and peace will be with you from God the Father and from the LORD Jesus Christ, the Son of the Father, in truth and love." We are always surrounded by grace and mercy. Peace is our companion. They are gifts from God.

Chapter 6

1. "My heart is severely pained within me, and the terrors of death have fallen upon me" (Ps. 55:4). David knew what it was like to be wracked by fears.

2. "Search me, O God, and know my heart; Try me, and know my anxieties" (Ps. 139:23). The God who knows our hearts so well understands we get worried. He sees our fears.

3. "Whenever I am afraid, I will trust in You" (Ps. 56:3). Notice how David says, "whenever." He doesn't deny the fact he's been afraid, and he knows fear will strike his heart again. God doesn't say he'll protect us from being afraid, but He promises that when we are fearful, He'll be worthy of our trust.

4. "You shall not be afraid of the terror by night, Nor of the arrow that flies by day" (Ps. 91:5). In other words, we don't need to be afraid of the things that go "bump in the night"—figments of our imagination and borrowed troubles. And, we don't need to worry about the dangers our day might hold. "He will not be afraid of evil tidings; His heart is steadfast, trusting in the LORD" (Ps. 112:7). We don't need to worry about bad news. "Therefore do not worry, saying 'What shall we eat?' or 'What shall we drink?' or 'What shall we wear?'" (Matt. 6:31). God's got the necessities covered. And lastly, Jesus' very quotable quote: "Therefore do not worry about tomorrow, for tomorrow will worry about its own things. Sufficient for the day is its own trouble" (Matt. 6:34).

5. "Do not fret because of evil doers" (Ps. 37:1). It must have been very good advice, because Solomon included it among his proverbs (Prov. 24:19).

6. "Anxiety in the heart of man causes depression, But a good word makes it glad" (Prov. 12:25). Constant worry can haul us downwards into depression. Conversely, fear can be driven away quite easily. All that is needed is a good word from a friend.

7. "Say to those who are fearful-hearted, 'Be strong, do not fear! Behold, your God will come with vengeance, With the recompense of God; He will come and save you'" (Is. 35:4). You can remind those who are afraid that God is near. You can bring good words of encouragement to their ears.

8. "In God (I will praise His word), In God I have put my trust; I will not fear. What can flesh do to me?" (Ps. 56:4). No matter what might come—struggles, disease, conflict, death—none of it can really touch the part of us that will live forever. This life, with all its worries, is only temporary. We must remember it will pass. Keep trusting God.

9. "Peace I leave with you, My peace I give to you; not as the world gives do I give to you. Let not your heart be troubled, neither let it be afraid" (John 14:27). Set aside worry and fear, and accept Jesus' gift of peace.

Chapter 7

1. "I'm tired of all this—so tired. My bed has been floating forty days and nights on the flood of my tears. My mattress is soaked, soggy with tears" (Ps. 6:6 MSG). He's tired of it all—sick of it.

2. "A cheerful disposition is good for your health; gloom and doom leave you bone–tired" (Prov. 17:22 MSG). In the *New King James Version*, the same verse reads, "A broken spirit dries the bones." The *New Living Translation* says, "A cheerful heart is good medicine, but a broken spirit saps a person's strength."

3. "For the shepherds have become dull–hearted, And have not sought the LORD" (Jer. 10:21). "For the hearts of this people have grown dull. Their ears are hard of hearing, And their eyes they have closed, Lest they should see with their eyes and hear with their ears, Lest they should understand with their hearts and turn, So that I should heal them" (Acts 28:27). Sometimes, we know we are doing wrong, but we'd rather not change. So we shut our ears and shut our eyes to the truth, and in so doing, we become dull. And in Hebrews 5:11, the writer accuses the people of becoming dull of hearing because they have not grown, having refused to "exercise their senses" and move on from milk to meat.

4. "I am weary with my crying; My throat is dry; My eyes fail while I wait for my God" (Ps. 69:3). "I'm hoarse from calling for help, Bleary–eyed from searching the sky for God" (MSG). "I am exhausted from crying for help; my throat is parched and dry. My eyes are swollen with weeping, waiting for my God to help me" (NLT).

5. "Meanwhile, the moment we get tired in the waiting, God's Spirit is right along-side helping us along. If we don't know how or what to pray, it doesn't matter. He does our praying in and for us, making prayer out of our wordless sighs, our aching groans" (Rom. 8:26 MSG). The Holy Spirit helps us through periods of waiting and helps us to pray in the midst of them. He communicates our feelings to God when we can't find the words to describe them.

6. "For I will pour water on him who is thirsty, And floods on the dry ground; I will pour My Spirit on your descendants, And My blessing on your offspring" (Is. 44:3).

7. "I'll refresh tired bodies; I'll restore tired souls" (Jer. 31:25 MSG). In another translation, this verse reads, "I have satiated the weary soul, and I have replenished every sorrowful soul."

8. "Are you tired? Worn out? Burned out on religion? Come to me. Get away with me and you'll recover your life. I'll show you how to take a real rest. Walk with me and work with me—watch how I do it. Learn the unforced rhythms of grace. I won't lay anything heavy or ill–fitting on you" (Matt. 11:28–29 MSG). Jesus offers the weary a place of rest.

9. "I would have lost heart, unless I had believed That I would see the goodness of the LORD in the land of the living" (Ps. 27:13). Waiting will not last forever. No matter how long you've been drifting in the doldrums, God is able to send a fresh breeze.

Chapter 8

1. "My heart pants, my strength fails me; As for the light of my eyes, it also has gone from me" (Ps. 38:10). David's giving up because he's tired and he cannot see any hope. He's weak and thirsty, lifeless under the weight of his cares. In Psalm 55:5, David uses "fearfulness," "trembling," and "horror" to describe his emotional state. "My flesh and my heart fail" (Ps. 73:26). Without God's strength to buoy us, we are sure to lose heart.

2. "My heart is in turmoil and cannot rest; Days of affliction confront me" (Job 30:27). Job's afflictions brought on feelings of turmoil and restlessness. He is "troubled and restless" (NLT), "upset" (NCV), and his "stomach's in a constant churning, never settles down" (MSG).

3. "I am feeble and severely broken; I groan because of the turmoil of my heart (Ps. 38:8). *The Message* puts David's prayer a bit more picturesquely, "I'm on my last legs; I've had it—my life is a vomit of groans." Other versions use such colorful adjectives as "weak" and "faint" (NCV), "exhausted," "completely crushed," and "anguished" (NLT), "sore" (KJV), "benumbed" and "badly crushed" (NASB).

4. "For innumerable evils have surrounded me; My iniquities have overtaken me, so that I am not able to look up; They are more than the hairs of my head; Therefore my heart fails me" (Ps. 40:12). David is on the verge of losing heart because all of his troubles have overwhelmed him. They "pile up so high I can't see my way out" (NLT). He "cannot see a way of escape" (NCV). "Troubles ganged up on me, a mob of sins past counting. I was so swamped by guilt I couldn't see my way clear" (MSG). And because of it, David's "heart gave out" (MSG) and he said, "I have lost all my courage" (NLT).

5. "A prayer of the afflicted, when he is overwhelmed and pours out his complaint before the LORD. Hear my prayer, O LORD, And let my cry come to You" (Ps. 102:1). David turned to God when he was overwhelmed. He prayed to the LORD and poured out his heart to Him when he had nowhere else to turn.

6. "From the end of the earth I will cry to You, When my heart is overwhelmed; Lead me to the rock that is higher than I" (Ps. 61:2). We don't have to try to pull ourselves together before facing our LORD. Even if we've wandered to the very ends of the earth, God will hear our call. He will lead us to the place where we should have been. David asks God to lead him to the rock that is higher. We need something more, something greater, something stronger than ourselves when we are overwhelmed. We need God.

7. "Teach me Your way, O LORD; I will walk in Your truth; Unite my heart to fear Your name" (Ps. 86:11). What an interesting choice of words! I love the contrast between how scattered our hearts and feelings can become and David's plea for God to unite his heart.

8. "Blessed is the man whose strength is in You, Whose heart is set on pilgrimage" (Ps. 84:5). This is such a sweet verse. When we talk of staying focused and having purpose, we can think of David's psalm here. We set our hearts on a pilgrimage. The path stretches before us, and we pursue that way, no matter what distractions try to lure us off track.

Chapter 9

1. "The foolishness of a man twists his way, And his heart frets against the LORD" (Prov. 19:3). When we push ourselves away from the LORD in this way, we're being foolish. We know in our heart of hearts that God's way is good. But we also know His way isn't always easy. Resisting a change can have serious consequences. *The Message* is predictably blunt: "People ruin their lives by their own stupidity, so why does God always get blamed?"

2. "Perversity is in his heart, He devises evil continually, He sows discord" (Prov. 6:14). Our hearts "plot evil" (NLT), "stir up trouble" (NLT), "start arguments" (NCV), "spread strife" (NASB), "devise mischief" (KJV), and are "cooking up something nasty" (MSG).

3. "A man will be commended according to his wisdom, But he who is of a perverse heart will be despised" (Prov. 12:8). *The Message* translates this proverb, "A person who talks sense is honored; airheads are held in contempt." Other translations call the perverse person "stupid" (NCV) and "warped" (NLT), and agree that this person will get no R.E.S.P.E.C.T. (thank you, Aretha) and be despicable (thank you, Daffy Duck).

4. "Those who are of a perverse heart are an abomination to the LORD, But the blameless in their ways are His delight" (Prov. 11:20). In other words, "God can't stand deceivers" (MSG). No believer really wants to hang onto the contrariness in his or her heart. It is a relief to let go of rebellion and accept God's Word. There is certainly good motivation to do so in this proverb, for none of us wish to be an abomination before the LORD.

5. The reality of living contrary to God is that we are fooling ourselves. We think what we are building is fine and beautiful and satisfying, but in reality it is like a house of cards, doomed to fall. Is it the result of clinging to our rebellious ways? One day, God will force us to face the truth, and the reality check will leave us stunned. We will regret the time we wasted in worthless pursuits, the lost opportunities to give glory to God, and the painful consequences of our perversity. Perhaps then, we will wish we had been more receptive, more teachable, less stubborn, and less determined to go our own way.

6. "In accordance with your hardness and your impenitent heart you are treasuring up for yourself wrath in the day of wrath and revelation of the righteous judgment of God" (Rom. 2:5). We look around and see all kinds of sin in the world. It's socially acceptable to do all manner of wickedness, and most people don't care one bit what God's perspective might be. When we harbor sin in our contrary moods, we're just as bad as the rest of the world, for sin is sin. Don't cling to things with an unrepentant heart. Don't let hardness prevent you from hearing the Spirit's quiet urging. Such behavior only stirs up God's wrath against sin.

7. "See, O LORD, that I am in distress; My soul is troubled; My heart is overturned within me, For I have been very rebellious" (Lam. 1:20). When we recognize the rebellious streak in our hearts, we are urged to be honest before the LORD. After all, He is the only one who can help us!

8. e, b, f, c, g, a, d

9. "Since we respect our earthly fathers who disciplined us, should we not all the more cheerfully submit to the discipline of our heavenly Father and live forever?"

(Heb. 12:9 NLT). We need to trust our Heavenly Father, submitting cheerfully to Him. After all, that is the path to eternal life.

Chapter 10

1. As each month passes, we are given a fresh opportunity to show a steadfast spirit. It's so much easier to snip and grouse and sulk and groan, but we don't have to be ruled by our tumbled feelings. God doesn't necessarily ask us to take on great things when we are feeling our weakest, but He gives us the chance to pull through with grace.

2. "As a face reflects in water, So the heart reflects the person" (Prov. 27:19 NLT). "Just as water mirrors your face, so your face mirrors your heart" (MSG).

3. "These people draw near to Me with their mouth, And honor Me with their lips, But their heart is far from Me" (Matt. 15:8). Jesus wasn't flattered by the friendliness of the Pharisees. He knew the blackness of their hearts and the cruel intentions hidden there.

4. "Out of the abundance of the heart the mouth speaks. A good man out of the good treasure of his heart brings forth good things, and an evil man out of the evil treasure brings forth evil things" (Matt. 12:34–35). When we think and say things for which we are ashamed later, it brings to the surface the needs in our hearts.

5. A woman who has a self–willed heart acts out of purely selfish motives. When considering what to do, her first thoughts are: *What do I want. What would I like. What do I feel like doing.* When a heart is God–willed, it means a woman has given God first place in it. Before she acts or reacts, she considers God's wishes in the situation. She acts on His behalf, as His emissary, as His servant in all things.

6. Paul wanted to live in such a way that Jesus would be revealed in him. Is that your prayer? Do you want people to look at you and see the changes wrought by Christ? Does your heart, which belongs to Jesus, shine forth clearly—even when you're not in the mood?

7. "Like one who takes away a garment in cold weather, And like vinegar on soda, Is one who sings songs to a heavy heart" (Prov. 25:20). Another version reads: "Singing cheerful songs to a person whose heart is heavy is as bad as stealing someone's jacket in cold weather or rubbing salt in a wound" (NLT).

8. Solomon talks about loud women, unwise women, foolish women, nagging women, quarrelsome women, complaining women, contentious women, and women who lack discretion. It's not hard to tear things down around us when we have been called instead to build up. Just because we're "not in the mood" to do the right thing doesn't give us the excuse to act foolishly. When we do good, in spite of the difficulty, we are wise.

9. d, j, a, f, h, b, i, n, l, e, m, g, c, k

Chapter 11

1. Paul describes the ungodly as "hopelessly confused" (Eph. 4:17 NLT). They have shut their minds and hardened their hearts to God, and don't care about right or wrong. All they care about is what feels good. Paul reminds us we are no longer like this. Our minds and spirits have been renewed, and God leads us into righteousness and holiness.

2. "When He looked out over the crowds, His heart broke. So confused and aimless they were, like sheep with no shepherd" (Matt. 9:36 MSG). Jesus looked at the people, and His heart ached for them. He could see how lost and confused they were.

3. "We're all like sheep who've wandered off and gotten lost. We've all done our own thing, gone our own way" (Is. 53:6 MSG). We get lost when we try to do things our own way. Sheep without a shepherd are underfed, afraid, dismayed, and lacking, according to Jeremiah 23:4. And Jeremiah 50:6 describes the lost sheep this way: "they wandered aimless through the hills. They lost track of home, and couldn't remember where they came from" (MSG).

4. "Should I wander off like a lost sheep—seek me! I'll recognize the sound of your voice" (Ps. 119:176 MSG). The psalmist says if he becomes lost, he wants God to look for him, come after him. The lost sheep calls for the help of its shepherd.

5. "The Son of Man came to find and restore the lost" (Luke 19:10 MSG). Lost in sin, lost along the way, lost in doubts or fears, lost in an emotional whirlwind—it doesn't matter. Jesus can find you.

6. "I'll go after the lost, I'll collect the strays, I'll doctor the injured, I'll build up the weak ones and oversee the strong ones so they're not exploited" (Ezek. 34:16 MSG).

7. c, e, a, f, d, b

8. "There is a way that seems right to a man, But its end is the way of death" (Prov. 14:12). Solomon reminds us again that we cannot trust our own instincts because our heart is deceitful. Isaiah says when we are allowing God to lead us, "You ears shall hear a word behind you, saying, 'This is the way, walk in it,' Whenever you turn to the right hand Or whenever you turn to the left" (30:21). And later in Isaiah, a Holy Road is described: "A highway shall be there, and a road. And it shall be called the Highway of Holiness. The unclean shall not pass over it, But it shall be for others. Whoever walks the road, although a fool, Shall not go astray" (35:8). Later, in verse 9, Isaiah says the redeemed shall walk there.

9. c, e, a, f, b, g, d

Chapter 12

1. "I know that nothing is better for them than to rejoice, and to do good in their lives" (Eccl. 3:12). Our emotions can throw us for a loop, but if our determination is always to do good, we won't get into so much trouble.

2. "Choose for yourselves this day whom you will serve...But as for me and my house, we will serve the LORD" (Josh. 24:15). When we face our options and deliberately place ourselves in the LORD's service, we are doing the right thing.

3. "Depend on the LORD and His strength; always go to Him for help" (Ps. 105:4 NCV). Or as the *New King James Version* puts it, we need to "Seek the LORD and His strength." We are often proven feeble in resisting our sinful inclinations, but God is an everlasting source of strength. It is to Him we should turn. It is upon Him we must depend.

4. "I depend on Christ's mighty power that works within me" (Col. 1:29 NLT). Paul's ministry was not an easy one by any means. The only way he could accomplish God's purpose for his life was through the strength God supplied. God offers us that same resource—strength to do His will.

5. c, e, a, f, b, d

6. "That Christ may dwell in your hearts through faith; that you, being rooted and grounded in love, may be able to comprehend with all the saints what is the width and length and depth and height—to know the love of Christ which passes knowledge; that you may be filled with all the fullness of God" (Eph. 3:17–19). Of course we must have emotions. How could God's people understand a God who is love, if we could not feel love? We have these emotions because God made us a little like Himself. We feel because He feels. The only reason we get so muddled is because sin gets in our way.

7. "As each one has received a gift, minister it to one another, as good stewards of the manifold grace of God" (1 Pet. 4:10). We are to be good stewards of our emotions, using them to minister to one another.

8. Isaiah tells us we must "learn to do good" (Is. 1:17). "As we have opportunity, let us do good to all, especially to those who are of the household of faith" (Gal. 6:10). Doing good must become our way of life. It touches every person we meet. "Do not forget to do good and to share, for with such sacrifices God is well pleased" (Heb. 13:16). God knows doing good is not easy for us. Why else would He consider it a sacrifice?

9. "Let us not grow weary while doing good, for in due season we shall reap if we do not lose heart" (Gal. 6:9). Hang in there, sister! Don't lose heart!

✦ ACKNOWLEDGMENTS ✦

© Clairmont, Patsy, *The Best Devotions of Patsy Clairmont,* (Grand Rapids, MI: Zondervan Publishing House, 2001)

© Clairmont, Patsy. *The Hat Box* (Nashville, TN: W Publishing Group, 2003).

© Clairmont, Patsy. *Sportin' a 'Tude* (Colorado Springs, CO: Focus on the Family Publications, 1996).

© Clairmont, Patsy; Johnson, Barbara; Meberg, Marilyn; Swindoll, Luci. *The Joyful Journey* (Grand Rapids, MI: Zondervan Publishing House, 1998).

© Clairmont, Patsy; Johnson, Barbara; Meberg, Marilyn; Swindoll, Luci. Walsh, Sheila; Wells, Thelma. *We Brake or Joy!* (Grand Rapids, MI: Zondervan Publishing House, 1998).

© Johnson, Barbara. The Best Devotions of Barbara Johnson (Grand Rapids, MI: Zondervan Publishing House, 2001).

© Johnson, Barbara, *Daily Splashes of Joy,* (Nashville, TN: W Publishing Group, 2000)

© Johnson, Nicole, *Fresh–Brewed Life: A Stirring Invitation to Wake up Your Soul,* (Nashville, TN: Thomas Nelson, Inc., 2001)

© Johnson, Nicole, *Keeping a Princess Heart in a Not-So-Fairy-Tale World*, (Nashville, TN: W Publishing Group, 2003)

© Meberg, Marilyn, *The Best Devotions of Marilyn Meberg* (Grand Rapids, MI: Zondervan Publishing House, 2001)

© Swindoll, Luci. The Best Devotions of Luci Swindoll (Grand Rapids, MI: Zondervan Publishing House, 2001).

© Swindoll, Luci, *I Married Adventure* (Nashville, TN: W Publishing Group, 2003)

© Walsh, Sheila, *The Best Devotions of Sheila Walsh and Unexpected Grace* (Grand Rapids, MI: Zondervan Publishing House, 2001)

© Wells, Thelma, *The Best Devotions of Thelma Wells* (Grand Rapids, MI: Zondervan Publishing House, 2001)

✦ STATEMENT OF FAITH ✦

*W*omen of Faith believes...

The Bible to be the inspired, the only infallible, inerrant Word of God.

There is one God, eternally existent in three persons: Father, Son, and Holy Spirit.

He has revealed Himself in creation, history and Jesus Christ.

God's creation of the world and humankind with humanity's rebellion and subsequent depravity.

In the person and work of Jesus Christ, including His deity,

His virgin birth, His sinless life, His true humanity, His miracles,

His substitutionary death, His bodily resurrection,

His ascension to heaven, and His personal return in power and glory.

That for salvation of the lost, sinful man, regeneration by the Holy Spirit is absolutely essential.

Salvation is by grace through faith in Christ as one's Savior.

In the present ministry of the Holy Spirit by whose indwelling the Christian is enabled to live a godly life and to grow in the knowledge of God and Christian obedience.

In the resurrection of both the saved and the lost—the saved unto the resurrection of life and the lost unto the resurrection of damnation.

In the spiritual unity of believers in the LORD Jesus Christ and in the importance of church for worship, service and missions.

✦ NOTES ✦

✦ Notes ✦

✦ Notes ✦

✦ NOTES ✦

THE COMPLETE WOMEN OF FAITH®
STUDY GUIDE SERIES

RECEIVING GOD'S LOVE
FOREWORD BY PATSY CLAIRMONT

CULTIVATING CONTENTMENT

ADVENTUROUS PRAYER
FOREWORD BY PATSY CLAIRMONT

MANAGING YOUR MOODS

LIVING ABOVE WORRY AND STRESS

KNOWING GOD'S WORD
FOREWORD BY LUCI SWINDOLL

LIVING IN JESUS

LIVING A LIFE OF BALANCE
FOREWORD BY MARILYN MEBERG

A LIFE OF WORSHIP

GIVING GOD YOUR ALL

ENCOURAGING ONE ANOTHER
FOREWORD BY NICOLE JOHNSON

DISCOVERING GOD'S WILL FOR YOUR LIFE
FOREWORD BY SHEILA WALSH

WOMEN OF FAITH®

To find these and other inspirational products, visit www.nelsonimpact.com.

A Message of Grace & Hope
for Every Day

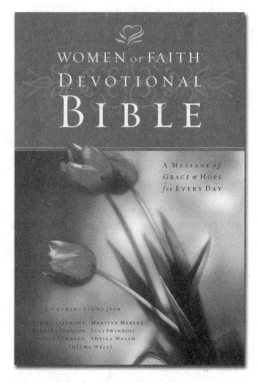

Hardcover: 0-7180-0378-0
Paperback: 0-7180-0377-2
Bonded Leather: 0-7180-0379-9

The *Women of Faith*® *Devotional Bible* provides women with the inspiration and resources needed to strengthen their walk with God and build stronger relationships with others. It helps women of all ages and stages in life – mature believers and those who have yet to believe, from all backgrounds, church and non-churched — to grow spiritually, emotionally, and relationally.